Selling in the Age of AI

A Playbook for Modern Sales Success

Soulaima Gourani

Soulaima Gourani

First published Soulaima Gourani - 2024

Copyright © 2025 Soulaima Gourani

All rights reserved. No part of this publication may be copied or reproduced in any form, by any means, electronic or otherwise, without prior consent from the copyright owner and publisher of this book.

First edition

Table of Contents

Introduction *4*

Future of sales *12*

Shift from selling to consulting: *32*

Be better at humans *46*

Map out your current network *56*

Expand your network *59*

Successful contact with new clients *63*

Caring for (new) client relationships *72*

Loyal relationships (test the waters) *76*

Networking situations *79*

Sales and marketing in the year 2030 .... *100*

10 Trends shaping 2030 and 5 strategies for client-centered success *103*

Introduction

The future isn't just built by great ideas - it's built by those who bring those ideas to the people who need them. Whether you realize it or not, you're selling every day. You're selling ideas, projects, products - or even yourself. Yet, while sales skills are critical to success across nearly every profession, most people have never learned to sell effectively. This isn't just a minor gap; it's a hidden crisis that silently limits careers, stifles innovation, and slows business growth.

Sales will exist for as long as there are people, but the craft itself is undergoing profound transformation. Mastering sales in today's world doesn't mean adopting a traditional salesperson role; it's about building trust, solving meaningful problems, and creating real value - skills that will only become more vital as AI reshapes the landscape.

My journey began in 1999 when I crossed paths with a visionary founder and CEO of a software company in Norway. At the time, I was an intern at the Danish embassy in Oslo.

This CEO saw something in me: a knack for making connections, building trust, and bringing people together. So, he took a chance and invited me into his organization, giving me my first role in tech.

I was an odd candidate. I'd been kicked out of school in 7th grade, completed some trade school, and worked gritty jobs like cell phone sales, night cleaning, and fitness instruction. I had no background in tech, but my work ethic was unbreakable, and I quickly found my strength in building trust and creating a network of allies. I found I could navigate the complexity of large organizations, identifying decision-makers, understanding the undercurrents, and tapping into the chain of influence. These skills allowed me to make historic deals and lay the foundation of my career from 2000 to 2004. I performed so well that, in my second year on the job, I closed one of the largest software deals in Scandinavia - all I had was a vision, a string of code, and one developer by my side.

When I returned to Denmark after a few years in Norway, I faced a daunting challenge: opening a Danish office for our Norwegian company from scratch. I had no network, no contacts, and no reputation. I'd left Denmark as a student back in 1998, virtually unknown in professional circles. Now, I was back, sitting alone in an empty office, with the weight of building something from nothing.

With Easter around the corner, I decided to take an unconventional approach. I hand wrote notes to every CEO I could find an address for, each note paired with an Easter egg. My handwriting wasn't particularly impressive, but it was personal, genuine, and, most importantly, memorable. To my surprise, those handwritten notes sparked an unexpected response: coffee invites, open doors, and conversations I never anticipated.

Fast forward a year, and I found myself on the Copenhagen stock exchange stage, recognized as an emerging voice in Denmark's business community. I'd gone from virtually unknown to influential, all without relying on expensive network memberships, luxury cars, or lavish gestures and business dinners.

A few years later I accepted a new job and a huge challenge from Hewlett Packard (HP) to rebuild a fractured relationship with Microsoft. This wasn't just any partnership; HP and Microsoft had an FLP (Frontline Partnership) to drive collaborative deals and win market share from Dell. But by the time I joined, the connection had deteriorated. I was brought in to fix it, with a minimal budget, zero existing relationships at Microsoft, and a partnership on the ropes. I had no prior strategy to rely on and no one to turn to for guidance. I was thrown straight into the deep end!

Every Wednesday, I'd decided drive over to Microsoft's HQ and sit in their cafeteria, hoping to open doors. Initially, I was just "the HP person" - they weren't interested. After weeks of this, I tried something new. I brought a large jar of candy, placed my business card next to it, and each week, I'd refill the jar, grab a coffee, and wait.

Slowly, the candy sparked small connections, and casual chats grew into real conversations. Over time, this simple gesture built something powerful. Within a few months, I had gained Microsoft's trust to the point that I was issued my own access key to the building. Our teams began winning deals together, and a few people even thought I was a Microsoft employee. Today, many of those connections remain some of my most valuable in the industry. What did it take? Persistence, empathy, and a $20 jar of candy.

Many years later, I made the leap to Silicon Valley with a bold vision: to start my own software company. I arrived without a network, barely knew anyone well in the Valley, and had never built a software company from scratch before. But I had one critical asset - a plan. Before even seeking VC funding, I secured a letter of intent (LOI) from a company with over 10,000 employees, stating that if I could build this software, they'd buy it. That letter unlocked doors to top investors, positioning me as one of Silicon Valley's best-funded early-stage startups.

In 2024, we were named AI Product of the Year. Since 2022, we've won numerous awards and been featured on several prestigious podcasts and shows. This recognition was possible thanks to my distribution and PR skills.

Imagine landing in the world's most competitive ecosystem for software startups, fueled by nothing but ambitions —and succeeding. My advantage wasn't just the product; it was a strategy built on resilience, tactical relationship-building skills, and knowing how to build a community around a product.

I quickly assembled an advisory group of 15 of the world's most respected companies, inviting them to become VIP users and influencers in our development process. Companies like Hitachi Japan, IKEA, Siemens, Volvo, Novo Nordisk, and Maersk sat in the front row, shaping our software with their insights and validating our direction.

How did I achieve this? Through a genuine focus on community, building advocates, and creating a sense of belonging around something meaningful. This experience taught me a key insight about the startup world: many founders excel in creating products but struggle when it comes to distribution - or what I like to call "strategic relationship building."

Early traction comes from forging partnerships and a fanbase that believes in and drives your vision forward. I've spent over two decades in the trenches - leading at companies like Maersk and HP and building tech ventures as a VC-backed entrepreneur in Silicon Valley.

Your business, no matter how brilliant, doesn't move forward unless someone buys in - whether it's a paying customer, an investor, or even a team member rallying behind the vision. Sales is not just a function; it's the engine of innovation and growth.

This book is the distillation of a lot of what I've learned. I'll share the methods, insights, and unconventional strategies that helped me close high-stakes deals and build lasting relationships in complex industries. This isn't about learning sales "tricks" or techniques; it's about pragmatic mastering the mindset and practices that make connections authentic and business successful.

Whether you're a founder, freelancer, or professional who's never thought of themselves as a "salesperson," the principles in this book are for you. If you apply these systems, you'll find that your approach to building relationships - and your impact - will evolve. Together, let's redefine what it means to be effective in sales, turning relationships into results in a way that's authentic, powerful, and sustainable. This book is for anyone who wants to build lasting commercial relationships that drive real impact and revenue. Whether you see yourself as a salesperson or not, this guide will help you master the skills to get your product, service, or idea into the hands of people who need it.

Sales isn't only for people with "sales" in their job title. It's a core skill for everyone. Founders need it to get early adopters. Leaders need it to inspire their teams. Engineers need it to evangelize their work. Whether you're raising capital or convincing your colleagues to support your project, selling is about influence - it's the art of getting people excited about your vision.

In my career, I've launched software products, deployed technology, and built relationships with clients across 50+ countries. I've authored three books and contributed to over 16 others. But the most important thing I've learned along the way is this: Relationships are everything. A loyal customer isn't just a buyer - they're an advocate, an evangelist, and ultimately, a fan who will sell on your behalf.

I want to give you the tools to thrive - even if you've never considered yourself a salesperson. You'll learn how to build connections that go beyond transactions, inspire trust, and generate loyalty. It's about turning your customers into superfans - because when people believe in what you do, they don't just buy; they tell everyone they know. The strategies in this book will help you navigate that game - not just to sell, but to create something that people love and can't stop talking about.

In a room full of students try to ask how many want to be in sales - maybe one hand goes up. But ask how many want to be entrepreneurs or top executives, and suddenly, it's a sea of eager hands. Here's the truth few realize success in powerful roles hinges on the very skill they're hesitant to embrace - sales.

Sales isn't about old-school pitches or pushing products. Every ambitious leader must "sell" - whether inspiring talent to join their mission, convincing investors to fund a bold vision, or turning customers into loyal fans. Research underscores this: 65% of startups fail due to weak sales and poor market fit, according to CB Insights.

Countless professionals lose out on career-defining opportunities simply because they lack the skills to communicate their value, gain buy-in, or move others to action. For those who don't identify as "salespeople," the challenge is even more pronounced. But here's the reality - sales aren't about "the hard sell." It's about unlocking the potential to influence, connect, and drive impact. Mastering sales means building trust, communicating value, and creating momentum that scales.

In this book, I'm sharing a toolkit for those who want to bridge this critical gap. Whether you're an entrepreneur, freelancer, or corporate professional, these insights will empower you to sell with confidence, purpose, and results - no title change required. Whether you're launching a company, scaling a team, or pursuing your next leadership role, this book will equip you to leverage the ultimate entrepreneurial skill - one that even the best doesn't know they need.

Sales isn't just about closing deals; it's about opening doors—to opportunities, relationships, and a better future for everyone. Let this book be your blueprint for becoming not just a great salesperson, but an extraordinary one.

> *".... distribution should be essential to the design of a product. Poor sales are the most common cause of failure for startups."*
>
> **Peter Thiel**

Future of sales

Imagine stepping into a world where every sale feels like a partnership, every pitch a tailored experience, and every customer interaction powered by cutting-edge insights. Welcome to sales in the age of AI, where innovation meets the timeless art of persuasion.

At its core, sales is about connection. From the ancient open-air markets of Lydia, where coins were first minted, to today's digital ecosystems, the process of selling has always been central to human progress. But now, technology is rewriting the rules, challenging us to think bigger, move faster, and engage smarter.

From Trading to Transforming

The story of sales began with simple trades, barter systems where goods were exchanged for mutual benefit. The invention of coinage in 640 B.C. marked a turning point, formalizing the value of goods and paving the way for markets as we know them. By the Industrial Revolution, sales had become an art form. Skilled salespeople emerged as key players, using persuasive tactics to meet the growing demand for goods.

Fast-forward to today, and the stakes have never been higher. Modern sales is no longer just about transactions, it's about relationships, insights, and creating value at every step. With AI and data analytics leading the charge, sales professionals are equipped with tools their predecessors couldn't have imagined.

The AI Revolution in Sales

Artificial intelligence is not just a buzzword—it's a game-changer. It empowers sales teams to:

- **Understand Customers Better:** AI analyzes behaviors, preferences, and purchase patterns, offering actionable insights into what customers want before they even know it.
- **Streamline Processes:** Tools like CRMs and sales automation systems free up time for salespeople to focus on building connections rather than wrestling with admin work.
- **Personalize at Scale:** Imagine reaching hundreds of potential customers with tailored messages that feel uniquely crafted for each one.

But with great power comes great responsibility. Ethical questions loom: How do we balance data-driven insights with genuine human connection? How do we ensure persuasion doesn't cross the line into manipulation? These are the challenges that sales professionals must navigate in this new era.

Becoming an AI-Empowered Sales Leader

So, how do you thrive in this new landscape? Start by asking yourself:

- **What is my purpose?** Passion and purpose are the engines of success. Without them, even the best tools won't keep you motivated.

- **Am I adaptable?** Sales in the age of AI demands flexibility. The ability to pivot strategies and embrace change is non-negotiable.
- **How can I add value?** Customers today expect more than just products—they want solutions, insights, and genuine care.

Turning Challenges into Opportunities

Sales have never been easy, and it's not supposed to be. But every challenge, from understanding customer needs to overcome competition is an opportunity to innovate and grow. AI doesn't replace the human touch; it enhances it, making us more effective, empathetic, and insightful.

Your Journey Starts Now

Sales in the age of AI is like training for the Olympic Games. The tools, data, and insights are your coaches, but it's your dedication, passion, and willingness to adapt that will make you a champion. Whether you're a seasoned salesperson or just starting out, remember: the future is being written today. Will you step up and lead?

Let's address the elephant in the room: by 2030, artificial intelligence will fundamentally reshape the sales profession as we know it. It already is. For many, this sparks a genuine concern - what does a future dominated by AI mean for sales jobs? But here's the truth: embracing AI isn't optional; it's essential. As technology rapidly disrupts traditional roles, it also opens doors to new ways of thinking about customer engagement, growth strategies, customer relations, and, ultimately, the way we engage, lead and compete. The question isn't if AI will change sales; it's how we adapt to leverage its power and stay ahead.

Sales, at its core, began as a journey of individual initiative - a subjective, instinct-driven art where sellers relied heavily on personal motivation and intuition to drive results. In this early stage, success was crafted by those able to connect meaningfully, yet the approach was inherently limited by its dependence on subjective methods, lacking the consistency or scalability necessary for exponential growth.

The next leap in sales was transformative: sellers began to harness AI-powered insights, providing them with next-best actions, strategic talk tracks, and streamlined workflows. This shift empowered sellers to operate with a new level of precision, shifting from reactive responses to proactive engagement. Sellers were no longer just closing deals; they were deploying data-driven strategies, creating relationships built on informed, real-time decisions. With AI as a trusted advisor, they could allocate their time and energy more effectively, investing in high-impact activities that yielded greater returns.

As mentioned in BCG-Executive 2024 we're entering an era that fundamentally reshapes how sellers operate within organizations. Real-time AI assistance and workflows are rewriting the rules of engagement. Instead of following set paths, sellers now adapt instantly within interactions, backed by continuous insights that guide them in the moment. This real-time intelligence redefines not only the seller's role but the entire structure of sales teams, fostering dynamic, responsive organizations capable of thriving in complex, competitive environments.

In this current evolution, AI-driven agents take the reins on routine tasks - prospecting, nurturing, and engaging 24/7, autonomously creating a seamless customer journey. These agents bring scalability, handling initial customer interactions and alerting human agents only when nuanced, high-value engagement is required. By liberating sales teams from the routine, we empower them to focus on what truly matters: building relationships, solving challenges, and driving impact at scale.

This evolution in sales is not just about adopting new tools but about reimagining the potential of human and machine collaboration to unlock new growth frontiers. Sales is transforming from a transactional, reactive function to a strategic, predictive force that shapes the future of customer engagement.

> *"Entrepreneurship is an infinite game. And in this game, sales are the key to growth, scale, and long-term impact. "*
>
> **Reid Hoffman**

In September 2024, I hosted a delegation of World Economic Forum Young Global Leaders on an immersive learning journey, bringing them to the heart of Silicon Valley innovation. Over a week, we met with visionary executives and experts at Google,

PayPal, the INSEAD San Francisco Hub, and Stanford's Human-Centered AI Institute (HAI). At every stop, the message was clear and resonant: those of us who fail to embrace AI risk being replaced by those who do.

AI is incredibly effective at scaling routine interactions - automated emails, scheduled calls, and the like - but it doesn't yet possess the nuance required for truly meaningful, face-to-face engagement. An AI won't extend a handshake, or deliver that subtle, reassuring glance that signals genuine understanding. It's not meeting with your business partners or joining you for lunch to build trust in a way that only people can. In essence, while technology accelerates and enhances parts of the sales process, the human touch (still) remains irreplaceable.

The power of authentic connection, of relationship-building, is something uniquely human - and that's precisely where we add the most value. We're not just augmenting our processes with AI; we're freeing up the time and energy to do what only we can do: foster relationships that are built on trust, empathy, and mutual respect.

AI has made remarkable inroads into the sales landscape. Predictive analytics, for example, is transforming how we approach customer relationships.

AI can already figure out who you will connect well with or not (like dating) and can predict what your customer will want next, before even they know it. Just think of Temu and Amazon, they use AI in several ways, including:

- **Personalized recommendations**: Both Temu and Amazon use AI to analyze user browsing and purchase history to provide personalized product recommendations.
- **Demand forecasting**: Temu uses AI to forecast demand and optimize supply chains. The company employs a "next-gen manufacturing" model which uses consumer data and AI to forecast demand and optimize supply chains. It's an approach that lets Temu offer competitive prices by reducing costs associated with traditional retail models.

Businesses don't just respond to customer needs - they anticipate them. We're living in that world right now. AI has reached a point where it's fundamentally reshaping how companies interact with and understand their customers, empowering them to go beyond traditional sales tactics. This isn't just about tech upgrades; it's about a strategic transformation that's opening powerful new opportunities and challenges.

- The future of sales is about making strong connections, because people trust people.
- It's about having your own special information, like a secret recipe no one else has.
- And it's about building things you control, instead of borrowing someone else's (think data or location etc.)

In December 2024, I visited MercadoLibre's headquarters in Buenos Aires, Argentina. As Latin America's largest e-commerce platform, MercadoLibre has revolutionized online shopping and payments through cutting-edge AI integration.

Their AI enhances personalized recommendations, dynamic pricing, and fraud prevention in their payment platform, Mercado Pago. It also optimizes logistics and supply chains, improving efficiency and access for small businesses and entrepreneurs.

MercadoLibre's use of AI showcases how technology can drive growth, inclusion, and innovation in emerging markets, setting a powerful example for the future of e-commerce and financial services.

It's always struck me as odd that many companies place some of their lowest-paid and least-trained employees on the front lines of customer service, the critical point of interaction with their customers. This approach often undermines the quality of service and the overall customer experience.

With AI, companies have a unique opportunity to rethink this model. By automating repetitive tasks and freeing up resources, businesses can afford to invest more in their customer service and sales teams. This means better salaries, improved training, and a more motivated workforce, ultimately leading to friendlier and more effective service. It's a win-win for both companies and their customers.

Successful companies are those that master the balance of **high touch,** exceptional, personable service delivered by great people, and **high tech** - intuitive, user-friendly technology seamlessly integrated into the customer journey. Personally, I'm a huge fan of Lemonade, the insurance company that has nailed this approach, creating an AI experience that feels both innovative and genuinely human.

Since the release of ChatGPT in November 2022, few could have predicted the pace at which AI would evolve into a global phenomenon. In just a few short years, it has spawned thousands of startups and is fundamentally reshaping the way we live and work - including the world of sales.

AI adoption is rapidly transforming workplace functions. In sales, AI is generating automated leads, identifying high-potential prospects, and personalizing outreach at an unprecedented scale. Meanwhile, in legal teams, it's drafting and analyzing complex documents, saving countless hours of manual work. These advancements are just the beginning of what AI can accomplish.

The numbers are staggering: 30% of all dollars invested in startups are going into AI, fueling the rise of new companies that are reaching unicorn status at record speed. Companies like Eleven Labs, with its AI dubbing software, Harvey, a legal tech platform, and Glean, a workplace data platform, demonstrate how quickly AI-driven solutions are achieving scale and impact. For sales professionals, this AI revolution represents an inflection point. Success in this era will require leveraging these powerful tools not just to streamline processes, but to fundamentally rethink how you and your sales teams engage with customers. From generating leads to closing deals, AI is not just a tool, it's a catalyst for innovation, efficiency, and growth.

This is the moment to adapt, adopt, and lead. The companies and sales teams that embrace AI today will set the standard for success in the future.

In a recent move, Indian startup Dukaan laid off 90% of its support staff, replacing them with an AI-powered chatbot that cut response times from 1 minute 44 seconds to instantaneous and reduced issue resolution times by 98%. At the CEO Summit Shah explained that while the layoffs were "tough," they were crucial for profitability in today's economic climate. The AI integration slashed customer support costs by 85%, highlighting a shift where companies use AI to streamline operations, reduce overhead, and enhance customer experience.

This case underscores a major trend: as AI systems like chatbots take over routine, repetitive tasks, sales support jobs are at risk. AI's ability to handle tasks formerly done by people - especially in customer-facing roles, signals an evolving landscape for sales. The Organization for Economic Cooperation and Development (OECD) warns that AI may increasingly impact low- and middle-skilled jobs but will also affect professionals in high-skilled roles like finance, law, and medicine.

Today's AI doesn't just collect data - it learns from it. Algorithms now analyze vast data streams, like purchase history, online behavior, and social media activity, to identify patterns in customer behavior that would be invisible to the human eye. Think about the amount of data a company like Amazon processes every second: every click, every cart addition. AI understands each individual customer on a deeper level, allowing businesses to deliver hyper-relevant product suggestions and tailored marketing messages.

This goes far beyond a simple, "You might like this." AI can look at past behavior, current trends, and even data from similar customers to suggest the exact product that fits a customer's needs at just the right moment. This is the magic behind why your Spotify knows what you want to hear or why Netflix seems to have a sixth sense for your next binge-watch.

Then there's predictive analytics, a tool that's becoming indispensable across sectors. By analyzing historical data, AI can forecast customer behaviors with surprising accuracy. If you're in retail, this means knowing when a customer might need a refill on their favorite product. If you're in finance, it could mean identifying when a customer might be ready for a new service. Predictive analytics has transformed forecasting from a hopeful guess to a science. And here's where it gets even more strategic: customer churn prediction.

AI can detect subtle changes in behavior that signal when a customer may be on the verge of leaving. With this insight, companies can act before it's too late, deploying targeted retention strategies to keep customers engaged and loyal. This isn't just a lifeline for the customer relationship; it's a competitive advantage that can drive revenue and enhance customer lifetime value.

Some of the biggest names in the business world are already deploying AI in these ways. An e-commerce platform like Alibaba uses it to recommend products based on browsing and purchase history, enhancing user experience and increasing conversions. Retailers like Target are using AI to segment customers based on loyalty data, allowing them to create precision-targeted promotions that drive in-store traffic. And marketers are leveraging AI-driven insights to personalize campaigns down to individual behaviors, ensuring the right message reaches the right person at the right time.

AI-powered chatbots, once considered a novelty, are now capable of handling up to 85% of customer interactions. These bots are trained to answer questions, offer product recommendations, and even schedule follow-ups, allowing human sales teams to focus on high-stakes, high-value conversations. This shift isn't merely about efficiency; it's about amplifying human potential by letting

AI manages routine, repetitive tasks that don't require the human touch. The impact of AI on the sales funnel is no less transformative. Today's AI doesn't merely assist with sales; it actively shapes and optimizes the entire process, from prospecting to close. Advanced tools like Gong and Clari serve as silent team members, analyzing every customer interaction - from emails to calls to social media engagement - and turning these insights into actionable strategies. And the scale of AI's integration into sales isn't slowing down.

By 2030, it's expected that over 70% of customer interactions will rely on AI-driven insights, which makes adopting a data-first mindset not just a benefit but a necessity for survival in this new age.

Future of sales will demand a deep understanding of both how customers use AI and how sales teams can leverage it for a seamless, data-rich experience.

Experts agree: to thrive, sellers need to think like their buyers, using AI to create personalized, efficient interactions. Yet, while AI can streamline and enhance the process, it's the human connection that ultimately seals the deal. AI will empower sales professionals, but empathy, relationship-building, and adaptability will be what makes salespeople irreplaceable. Sales is shifting to meet these demands, favoring dynamic, cross-functional skill sets and tech-savviness over traditional roles. It's a thrilling time for sales - a profession evolving rapidly and offering exciting opportunities for those ready to harness both AI insights and authentic engagement.

As Marc Benioff, CEO of Salesforce, puts it, "We're entering the third wave of AI." This next phase of sales isn't about robots taking over; it's about smarter tools doing the heavy lifting, so salespeople can focus on what they do best: connecting, strategizing, and closing deals. Microsoft has introduced AI-powered tools like Microsoft Sales Copilot, designed to streamline sales processes by automating tasks, providing real-time insights, and offering personalized recommendations.

Be sure to check out Hunter.io for finding email addresses and GMass, a super smart tool for crafting and sending impactful emails efficiently. Both are great resources to elevate your outreach game! **Scary or exciting?**

Anyways, the below guide draws on extensive data and insights from McKinsey, providing a research-backed approach to building high-performing B2B sales teams that can adapt and thrive. To succeed, here are four foundational pillars that anyone in a sales-adjacent role should know:

1. Embrace Agility: Adapt to Your Customer's Preferred Channels: Sales isn't just about in-person meetings anymore. Today, successful salespeople - and even those who never thought of themselves as salespeople - understand that adapting to the customer's preferences is essential. Some customers want virtual or WhatsApp meetings and calls, chats, e-mails or letters, while others expect in-person interactions.

The key is to be flexible and make the "highest and best use" of each customer's time. For instance, hybrid meetings now allow you to bring in experts and advisors virtually, enriching the conversation and providing immediate value to clients. If you're pitching your startup to investors or meeting new clients, offering them options for how to meet - whether it's over Zoom or in-person - shows respect for their time and positions you as flexible and considerate.

2. Get Comfortable with Data: Insights Are Your Competitive Advantage: Data isn't just for analysts; it's a tool every salesperson should be using to make informed decisions. The best salespeople don't just rely on instinct - they use data to pinpoint which prospects to focus on, what offers are most appealing, and which messages are likely to resonate. Fast-growing companies are investing in analytics that provide real-time customer insights, allowing them to tailor their approach to each client.

Why it matters for you: If you're new to sales, learning how to interpret and act on data will give you an edge. Data can tell you which leads are most promising, when to reach out, and even how to adjust your messaging to be more relevant. This kind of insight-driven approach can save you time and dramatically increase your effectiveness.

3. Use Technology to Make Selling Easier, Not Harder: Today's sales tools are designed to streamline your workflow, so you can spend less time on administrative tasks and more time building relationships. Whether it's a simple CRM for tracking customer interactions or AI tools that suggest the best next step for a deal, the right technology can make a huge difference. But don't get bogged down - start small, learn the basics, and focus on tools that solve specific problems.

Why it matters for you: If you're a founder juggling multiple roles or a new sales exec, using tech to automate routine tasks (like follow-ups or email sequences) will free you up to focus on what matters most: closing deals and building connections.

4. Invest in Learning: Sales is a Skill, and Skills Can Be Learned: Whether you're a seasoned pro or just starting out, sales is a skill that can be developed. The best salespeople today are constantly learning - whether it's understanding the latest trends, practicing negotiation techniques, or getting feedback from mentors. Companies with fast revenue growth prioritize continuous training for their sales teams, and the same mindset can work for you.

Why it matters for you: Embrace a growth mindset. Seek out resources like online courses, attend webinars, or shadow someone in your network who's skilled at sales. Sales is a craft, and like any craft, it gets easier (and more successful) the more you practice.

If you're looking to get ahead in today's fast-paced market, start by clarifying your role in sales, even if it's informal. Recognize the "sales" part of your job - whether it's building a brand, growing a customer base, or rallying a team around your vision. Embrace the tools and tactics available to you, and don't be afraid to dig into data or test new approaches. Recognize your wins along the way, even the small ones - they're signs you're getting better.

In a world where almost, every role involves some form of selling, those who learn to sell effectively - using insights, agility, and continuous learning - will find themselves with a serious advantage. In sales, action is everything, so start now.

Of course, the future isn't entirely bright for all sales roles. Some positions, particularly those centered on routine, transactional interactions like telemarketing, are at high risk. Recent research forecasts the potential loss of over one million sales jobs by 2030 as automation takes over these routine tasks. But this shift doesn't spell the end of sales; it signals a transformation in the skills needed to excel.

In the AI-driven landscape, high-level interpersonal skills - like empathy, strategic thinking, and nuanced negotiation - will become invaluable. While AI can analyze data and anticipate needs, it can't forge genuine human connections or navigate complex emotions. In fact, roles that emphasize emotional intelligence are among the least likely to be impacted by automation, underscoring a critical insight: the future of sales belongs to those who can blend AI with uniquely human skills.

Rather than replacing salespeople, AI offers an opportunity to redefine what it means to be a modern sales leader. Sales professionals now have the chance to become "AI orchestrators," seamlessly integrating technology with human creativity and intuition. With AI-powered insights, sales teams can tailor strategies, perfect timing, and personalize messages at an unprecedented level of precision. Those who harness AI's potential will enjoy a strategic advantage that pure human intuition simply can't replicate. Imagine a sales rep who can predict a client's needs based on real-time data analysis - no guesswork, just informed, targeted action. In a world increasingly driven by data, sales professionals who can combine AI's precision with their own insight will lead the industry forward.

In this AI-powered future, the role of a sales professional isn't diminished; it's enhanced. AI is more than just a tool - it's a partner that, when used effectively, has the potential to revolutionize careers and redefine what's possible in sales. For today's ambitious leaders, mastering the art of combining human intuition with AI-driven precision will be the defining skill of tomorrow's most successful sales teams.

Embracing AI isn't about abandoning traditional skills; it's about amplifying the unique human capabilities that make sales an irreplaceable craft. The real winners in this new landscape will be those who understand that the future of sales is not about replacing human talent but about elevating it.

In a world where generative AI (gen AI) frees up time for sellers to seek new markets. Imagine "Pranav," who works for a company that develops textile sensors that can be embedded into comfortable garments. His current sales accounts are mainly athletic-apparel companies, but gen AI helps him identify a new potential market: medical companies that can use the sensors to monitor and detect health issues. Gen AI develops a map for Pranav to expand his reach, detailing how he might approach new customers. Gen AI also generates a list of potential leads, prioritizing customers ready to enter the health-monitoring space. It then coaches Pranav on adjusting his sales approach according to the audience: when pitching to fitness companies, he focuses on customer testimonials; when pitching to medical companies, he focuses on data-driven insights

Personalization will deepen, moving away from one-size-fits-all to hyper-targeted, data-informed insights tailored for each client. Additionally, as remote and hybrid work reshape professional dynamics, virtual and immersive sales experiences will become standard, leveraging AR/VR for client engagement. In this evolving world, successful salespeople will be those who skillfully combine technology with empathy, trust-building, and adaptability to forge meaningful, lasting connections with clients.

Many people do not like the idea of selling, persuading, and influencing, but it is a part of most job descriptions. No matter what you do for a living, these skills are key for your future success. Trust me, without these skills, you won't succeed. At this point in history, things are quickly changing, especially the way we trade with one another. More than ever, you're expected to be able to work with and thrive in complex organizations, and you have to establish lasting relationships with clients and partners. Our ways of working together are being put to the test. Our work ranges from the physically visible and measurable kind to the more abstract and invisible kind that often take place inside our heads.

Your skills and abilities when it comes to thinking well are upgraded, informed, and strengthened by the quality of your relationships. You're living in a so-called networking society, which means that you're dependent on your knowledge and access to knowledge. The way you get this raw material is through your network. Your network is your ticket to creating value for your employer and your measure of higher value. You're probably working in a sector where your experiences, skills, and routines are constantly challenged. Your network is your access to influence, inspiration, and information. Your skills, routines, and experiences are at least a couple of days old and, therefore, not entirely fresh in your memory. Your knowledge ages faster nowadays than ever before.

Have you ever thought about how to ensure that you don't eliminate your knowledge and your market value? To maintain and develop your skills and market value, you must find a way to renew and adjust your knowledge so that you always know the right things at the right time.

You're in a stronger position when you're good at networking. Networking opens doors to gaining complementary knowledge from acquaintances when you're in a position where you need to solve a professional problem but you're coming up short by yourself, whether this is in terms of experiences, tools, or contacts. Your network helps to prepare you for change. Your network is the only guaranteed way to develop your skill sets. You can take as many courses and acquire as many degrees as you want, but at the end of the day, nothing beats a loyal and competent network. This is your access to compact knowledge and the direct path to individual and organizational results.

The good news!
AI isn't here to replace sales; it's here to augment it. Start by seeing AI tools as essential allies. Let AI handle routine tasks so you can focus on what matters: building real relationships and solving complex problems for your clients.

Shift from Selling to Consulting:

With AI streamlining many transactional aspects of sales, your role as a salesperson is shifting. You're not just a representative of a product; you're a consultant and a guide. Focus on uncovering the bigger problems your clients are facing and help solve them. Position yourself as the trusted advisor, the expert who provides strategic value beyond the immediate sale. In this era, clients need insightful guidance more than a sales pitch.

Double Down on Emotional Intelligence:
In a world of automation, it's your human skills that will differentiate you. AI may be fast, but it can't match genuine empathy or nuanced communication. Tune into the emotions and needs of your clients, and don't just listen - understand. In negotiations, resolving objections, and addressing complex concerns, empathy and the ability to read the room will always be your strongest assets.

Stay Agile and Responsive:
With AI accelerating decision-making, your customers are moving faster than ever. This means that as a salesperson, agility is everything. Be prepared to pivot quickly, engage at crucial points, and adapt as clients move swiftly through their decision-making process. The key is responsiveness, meeting the client where they are, exactly when they need you.

Commit to Lifelong Learning:
AI is constantly advancing, and so should you. Adaptability is your strongest edge, so make continuous learning a core part of your mindset. Experiment with new AI tools and strategies, stay curious, and embrace change as a constant. By remaining flexible and tech-savvy, you're positioning yourself as a forward-thinking sales professional in an industry that's evolving rapidly.

Every year, I spend between one and three weeks at universities around the world to study the latest technologies and trends. In 2024, I dedicated time specifically to deepening my understanding of AI. I spent a week at HKUST in Hong Kong, attended programs at INSEAD, Stanford HAI, and Universidad Torcuato Di Tella in Argentina. I also keep up with daily AI-focused podcasts and have assembled an AI sounding board of top experts from leading universities and professionals within my network, including those from Microsoft, Google, AWS, and other major institutions.

While I'm not an AI expert, I recognize the importance of staying informed - just as I did with the internet in the 90s or as I did with blockchain and crypto in 2021-2022.

Anyways, I returned to Denmark in 2001 after having spent some years living abroad in three other countries. I didn't know anyone on the Danish business scene when I arrived. I am half Danish, but all I had with me was the memory of how difficult it is to succeed in the country when you don't look like everyone else, when you weren't born into a powerful network, or when you didn't have the right last name. I remember how difficult things could be if you weren't a straight-A student or if you weren't among the white, Danish elite. I am a working-class girl, and I had to work my way up in life. I remember sitting in our new apartment in Copenhagen and thinking, How am I going to make this work? I don't know anyone and here I am, responsible for a brand-new company that nobody has ever heard of.

I pulled myself together and got to work, strategically networking my way through Denmark first, then the rest of Scandinavia, Europe, and the world. The client relationships I built then stand strong to this day. How?

Why value-based relationship sales?
The secret is "value-based relationship sales"! For so many years, professionals have operated on the assumption that clients are rational and relatively unaffected by emotions.

One group of people who have really taken this rational behavior to heart is specialists. Many seem unaffected by the fact that their arguments, studies, clinical data, and analyses are far from the only reasons that affect whether the client buys or doesn't buy their products and services.

While we like to think of sales as a logical, step-by-step decision process, research tells us otherwise. Studies show that up to 95% of purchasing decisions are made subconsciously, driven by emotions rather than reason. This means that despite having all the facts and figures, customers are often swayed by how a product or service makes them feel.

Sales isn't just about presenting the right information - it's about building connections, trust, and emotional resonance. It's these human elements that turn interest into commitment, often defying rational analysis

YOUR personality and attitude, not to mention the chemistry and trust between you and the client, is the deciding factor in whether the client buys and continues to buy from you, along with recommending you and your products and services to other people.

Studies show that around sixty percent of all failed sales meetings fail for two reasons, neither of which has to do with the product:

- The cultures of the two organizations and
- The chemistry between the seller and the buyer.

I was lucky a few years ago to study at Yale. Dhar, a professor at Yale, found that "emotions can significantly affect decision-making, sometimes even overruling logical analysis." His research shows that emotional appeals can prompt faster, more decisive actions from consumers, particularly when they feel positive about the product or brand. I also had the honor of attending a week's executive training at Cambridge. Research from Cambridge's Judge Business School delves into the psychological biases affecting decisions, especially in financial and sales contexts. Professor David Tuckett emphasizes that financial decisions are not made in a vacuum of logic; they are embedded in narratives and emotions that drive action. His studies reveal that consumers often create mental stories around products or investments, which can heavily influence buying behaviors beyond rational factors.

Are you talking to the heart or the head?
I did open for the EQ conversation, so now let us dive deeper into that! In so many sales situations, the seller focuses on the product and its wonderful characteristics. Even if you have the best product in the world, though, you have no guarantee that you'll achieve success among your clients. Many people overlook the importance of building, nourishing, and expanding their relationships with their clients. Even in cases where they don't overlook the importance, the attempt tends to be half-hearted.

Sales today isn't just about the pitch or a campaign; it's about creating meaningful emotional experiences that resonate deeply with consumers. Trust-building has taken center stage as we realize that a good sales experience is less about what's sold and more about how it makes people feel. Studies show that a staggering 95% of purchase decisions are driven by subconscious urges rooted in emotional responses - making this the ultimate leverage point for forward-thinking sales teams.

Peloton has mastered the art of emotional connection by transforming fitness from a solitary task into a dynamic, community-driven experience. Through personalized coaching, real-time shoutouts, and leaderboards that encourage friendly competition, Peloton engages users emotionally by creating a shared sense of purpose, achievement, and belonging. This sense of community keeps users motivated and fosters a deep loyalty to the brand, as users feel they're part of something bigger than just a workout routine.

Patagonia's approach goes beyond selling outdoor apparel; it's built an emotional connection with customers by aligning the brand with environmental activism and responsibility. By donating 1% of sales to environmental causes and promoting ethical sourcing, Patagonia appeals to consumers who value sustainability and environmental protection. This connection creates not just loyal customers but brand advocates who feel pride in supporting a brand that stands for the causes they believe in. For Patagonia, the product is only part of the story - their mission and activism resonate with customers on a personal and ethical level, fostering a deeply loyal customer base.

Both brands demonstrate that by tapping into consumers' emotions - whether through shared purpose or shared values - companies can transcend traditional sales, creating communities and advocates rather than mere buyers.

Take Apple, for instance. It doesn't just sell devices; it sells empowerment. Through its in-store and online experiences, Apple crafts an environment of discovery and delight, fostering a sense of belonging and innovation among users. It's why customers queue up before dawn for new releases - they're buying into a feeling, a lifestyle, not just a product. Another striking example comes from Salesforce's Trailblazer community. By connecting users emotionally to their purpose and broader professional goals, Salesforce goes beyond software, inviting its customers into a collaborative, purpose-driven space. Customers are emotionally invested in the brand because they feel a part of something bigger, a tribe united by common values.

Even AI is being harnessed to read and respond to customer emotions. Software companies use machine learning to analyze voice tone and sentiment during sales calls. They aren't just assessing the words spoken but the emotions behind them, tailoring responses to ensure buyers feel heard, understood, and valued. Research by Harvard Professor Gerald Zaltman shows that 95% of purchase decisions are made subconsciously, influenced by emotions rather than logic. Zaltman's work demonstrates that consumers primarily rely on feelings when deciding, even if they rationalize their choices afterward.

As Zig Ziglar once said, "If people like you, they'll listen to you, but if they trust you, they'll do business with you." In today's world, where customers are flooded with options, trust isn't just a nice-to-have - it's the foundation of a sustainable, fan-driven business.

Consider Simon Sinek's insight: "People don't buy what you do; they buy why you do it." It's no longer enough to just sell a product. Today's most successful businesses thrive connecting with their customers on a deeper, purpose-driven level. They're driven by a mission, a clear "why" that resonates with people and transforms them from passive buyers into active fans. When you focus on genuine human connection and shared values, you're not just creating customers - you're building a community of supporters who believe in what you stand for and are excited to champion your journey forward.

Positive Emotions Build Brand Loyalty
According to a study by the Journal of Consumer Research, positive emotional connections with a brand significantly impact loyalty, with 50% of consumers who feel emotionally connected to a brand willing to pay more for their products. This connection means customers are also 52% more likely to recommend the brand.

Customer Retention through Emotional Engagement
A Capgemini report found that customers with high emotional engagement levels are twice as likely to stay loyal to a brand and five times more likely to recommend it. This insight highlights how cultivating an emotional bond with customers can lead to a higher customer retention rate and overall brand advocacy.

Brands with High Emotional Engagement Outperform the Stock Market
HBR and Forrester report that brands with high emotional engagement outperform the stock market by over 20%. When customers connect emotionally with a brand, they're not only more likely to purchase, but they also increase overall brand value - a clear testament to the financial benefits of emotional engagement.

Personalization and Emotions in Digital Sales
Research from McKinsey shows that personalization, which taps into emotions by creating a sense of individual attention, can boost sales by 10-15%. Personalized interactions help companies build a rapport with customers, fostering positive emotional responses and increasing sales conversions.

Neuromarketing Shows Emotional Responses Lead to Action

Studies using fMRI technology have shown that ads and brand messages which evoke strong emotions activate the brain's amygdala (the region tied to emotions), leading to higher memorability and purchase intent. A Nielsen study found that ads with above-average emotional impact drive a 23% increase in sales.

Emotional Advertising Generates More Profits

A report by the Institute of Practitioners in Advertising (IPA) concluded that emotionally engaging ads perform nearly twice as well as rational ones, generating a 31% higher profit margin. Emotional ads build a deeper connection with audiences, leading to sustained sales boosts.

Storytelling and Emotional Impact on Sales

Research from Stanford University shows that stories are 22 times more memorable than facts alone, making storytelling a powerful emotional tool in sales. Companies that leverage storytelling in sales connect with customers on an emotional level, fostering trust and driving long-term loyalty.

Trust as a keystone

It's easier for two people to enter a business relationship when they trust each other personally and professionally and have a loyal, mutually beneficial relationship than it is for two people who are focused entirely on the product, rationality, and formality. In Denmark where I grew up, we have a tradition centered on not talking about our feelings, even though we know that clients use not only their heads but also their hearts and intuition when deciding whether or not to buy a product or service. A lot of people think the emotional side is too informal, fluffy, or unprofessional. Research shows that clients tend to buy more often or in higher quantities when three feelings are present in their relationship with the seller:

- **Trust**: The client needs to feel like they can count on you and that what they see and hear is what they'll get. In other words, they want to be sure that you're authentic.
- **Confidentiality**: What the client says, shows, and thinks must stay between the pair of you. There must be a level of mutual confidentiality and, for that to be possible, you need to have something personal to bring to the table, as well. The relationship needs to be informal.
- **Taken care of**: The client needs to feel that they're being taken care of. They need to feel that you're genuinely interested in helping them achieve success and that you'll take care of them in general.

Recent studies explore the ill-conceived notion that people act with complete rationality when it comes to decisions about money. Research found that, when we're handling money, we're relying primarily on the part of our brain that also manages emotions (better known as the insular cortex). The part of the brain that responds to different amounts of money is the same part of the brain that processes feelings. In other words, we're using the part of our brain that's meant for other tasks than making financial decisions. That's the main reason you shouldn't speak to your client's head; rather you should speak to their heart, and the best way is to establish value-based relationship sales.

So, as we move toward 2030, the most successful sales strategies will marry technological insights with the power of genuine human emotion. Brands that invest in these connections - through communities, tailored digital experiences, or emotionally intelligent sales practices - will stand out, building trust that goes far beyond the transaction.

Sales isn't just for salespeople; it's for anyone who wants to succeed. Entrepreneur Mark Cuban puts it best: "In business, you're always selling - to your prospects, investors, and employees. To be successful, learn to sell." Whether you're leading a startup, pitching ideas, or rallying a team, sales skills are the foundation of influence and impact.

Daniel Pink echoes this in To Sell Is Human, reminding us that "we're all in sales now." Learning to sell isn't about pushing products; it's about connecting, communicating, and inspiring others to believe in your vision. Embrace sales as a skill, and you'll unlock a world of possibilities - where your ideas resonate, your message is heard, and your career soars.

Imagine being a top athlete, tirelessly refining your craft to compete at the Olympic level. That's what mastering sales in today's hyper-dynamic, AI-driven marketplace feels like. It's not just a job, it's an art, a science, and a competitive arena where the best thrive. But unlike athletics, this game has no finish line.

Sales, at its core, is about people, understanding them, connecting with them, and solving their problems. The skills you hone here will be the superpower that propels your career and business forward.

Let's break it down: Sales is the lifeblood of every industry, from tech to retail. It's the engine that drives innovation and growth. And in an age where customers are savvier than ever, the stakes have never been higher.

Success in sales today isn't just about hitting quotas or making cold calls. It's about mastering a spectrum of skills that combine technical know-how with emotional intelligence. Whether you're negotiating multi-million-dollar deals or selling artisanal goods at a local market, the fundamentals are universal:

- **Communication:** Your words matter, but your tone and listening skills matter more. Customers don't just want to hear what you're selling, they want to feel understood.
- **Problem-Solving:** Your ability to diagnose a client's pain points and offer tailored solutions can make or break a deal.
- **Adaptability:** In an ever-changing marketplace, those who pivot quickly win. AI tools? Remote selling? Social selling? You've got to embrace it all.

Why Passion and Precision Matter
- Sales without passion is like a ship without a rudder. You might get somewhere, but it'll never be where you intended. When you're passionate, your enthusiasm becomes infectious. Clients sense it, trust it, and respond to it. Add precision—data-driven insights, well-honed skills, and you're unstoppable.

- Take negotiation, for example. A great negotiator isn't just persuasive; they're prepared, empathetic, and focused on creating win-win outcomes. Or consider active listening, it's not just about hearing but truly understanding your client's needs. These skills build trust, and trust closes deals.

A Day in the Life of a Modern Sales Pro
- Picture this: You start your day reviewing AI-generated insights about your top prospects. A quick glance at your CRM dashboard shows exactly where each client is in their journey. You customize your pitch with precision, knowing their pain points, preferences, and even their buying signals.
- In the afternoon, you meet with a client virtually, leveraging your consultative skills to discuss their challenges and offer tailored solutions. By evening, you've closed a deal, followed up with warm leads via automated emails, and reviewed analytics to refine your approach. Efficiency meets empathy, it's sales redefined.

The Sales Skills Checklist
Here's your guide to mastering the modern sales game:
1. **Active Listening:** Truly hear your clients and respond to their unspoken needs.
2. **Effective Communication:** Be clear, concise, and compelling.
3. **Problem-Solving:** Turn challenges into opportunities.
4. **Negotiation:** Aim for outcomes where everyone wins.
5. **Tech Savviness:** Leverage AI tools and CRM systems to supercharge your process.

Let's face it: sales aren't easy. Resistance to change, skill gaps, and misalignment between sales and marketing can derail even the best teams. But these are opportunities in disguise. The businesses that thrive are those that embrace change, invest in their people, and align their strategies.

Your journey might be unique, but the destination is clear: becoming the salesperson who not only meets but exceeds client expectations. Whether you're selling the latest tech or pitching a bold idea, remember this, sales is not just a job. It's a craft, a career, and a calling.

Be better at humans

At its core, sales aren't just about products or numbers; **it's about people.**

The ability to sell effectively hinges on building and leveraging relationships with the right people. To succeed, you must master the art of strategic networking - connecting with individuals who can champion your vision, open doors, and create opportunities that go beyond the immediate transaction.

In this section, I'll guide you through the strategies, mindsets, and tools that help you build an influential network from the ground up. You'll learn how to identify key players, foster meaningful connections, and become the kind of person people remember, trust, and recommend. Sales may be about closing deals, but your network is what gets you there.

As a foundational exercise in self-reflection, take a moment to consider: What truly motivates you in your work? Beyond targets, growth metrics, or accolades, what's the deeper passion that drives you to build, connect, and make an impact in this field?

Next, you need to network for three reasons:

- To do some good for yourself (your sales),
- To do some good for others (your clients and colleagues), and

- To contribute to your community (the big picture)

We know that people who take a goal-oriented approach to networking have easier access to inspiration, information, and influence, both at work and in their personal lives.

Companies that take a systematic approach to networking fare better than ones that don't. A study of 700 HR managers and CEOs from thirty-one industries and sixty-one countries show that companies that fare well financially, as measured by EBITDA, are fifty-seven percent more likely to use relationship tools and social networks than their counterparts that don't fare as well. The following bullet points are some facts to keep in mind:

- Nineteen percent of these companies regularly use networking as a tool for identifying individuals with relevant knowledge and relevant skill sets.
- Despite losses, twenty-one percent of these companies have recently increased spending on the resources required to improve relationships and networks.
- Twenty-seven percent of these companies use networking as a tool for expanding on innovative ideas.

Do you want direct access?
You're living in a society characterized by the oversaturation of information, limited amounts of concrete knowledge, rapid changes, and new needs and challenges. If you're working as a consultant to your clients and, therefore, have significant contact with them, chances are high that you'll meet with increasing pressure to create and maintain client relationships

to ensure that they develop a loyal and trusting relationship with you and the company.

Once you've established a strong network of competent individuals who are incredibly talented in areas where your own skills are lacking, you represent a broader area of knowledge than you do when you stand alone, and both your clients and your colleagues stand to benefit from that. In other words, you gain direct access to the previously inaccessible things that you and your company need.

The golden overview
Networking is a way of thinking and working; it's an activity. A network is a group of people with whom you have a special relationship. You can also be a formal member of a network or a networking group.

All your current relationships should be categorized to give you an overview of who you know, how well you know them, and how loyal you are to each other. This process is called strategic networking. Networking skills are all about mapping out who you know, nourishing the relationships you have, and expanding your circles by getting to know new people you need to know.

Motive and mission
To know who you need to know, you must determine where you and your company are headed. It's important to be conscious of your own needs if you want to take a targeted approach to networking. You need to be able to work on your networking motive and mission. The alternative is an unstructured and random networking tactic that will never produce great results.

The primary reason that people don't get what they want is that they don't know what they want. Ask yourself the following questions and give yourself concise answers:

- What is my overall networking mission?
- What are my commercial needs?
- What are the company's needs?

Archetypes

People tend to think that extroverts have an easier time networking than introverts, but there is no research that documents this assumed fact. The truth is that both archetypes have their strengths and weaknesses. Depending on the situation, people win or lose points for being extroverted or introverted. Which of the two are you?

You'll often hear that extroverts find it easier to gain success through others. In my experience, it's not as simple as that. When it comes to networking, there are obvious advantages to being an introvert. People with that personality type are great at one-on-one relationships and often get to know people on a deep level, which rarely happens for extroverts.

The fact of the matter is that a lot of extroverts are shy, just not in an expected way. It might be taboo, but you see it a lot, especially among leaders. They try to hide their shyness to the best of their abilities. If you happen to be shy around everyone, that shyness can lead to isolation within an organization, which tends to stand in the way when you present information about your company to receptions and other events. On the other hand, there are people out there who never get shy, which can also create a negative impression. Other people may assume you either lack self-recognition (reflection) or that other people don't mean all that much to you.

What you see below is an overview of the extroverted and introverted personality types, including the strengths they have and the challenges they face:

The Introvert's Strengths	The Extrovert's Strengths
Tend to be reflective and considerate	Find it easy to express thoughts and emotions
Are willing to make room for dialogue	Recharge during conversation
Spend time furthering relationships	Like meeting new people
Show loyalty and always have (a small number of) good, close relationships	Strive at navigating large groups of people and sizeable events
The Introvert's Challenges	**The Extrovert's Challenges**
Need more breaks; need to recharge social batteries before spending time with (unfamiliar) people	Can come across as superficial
Tend to hide in the background, making you easily misunderstood	Tend to race ahead when establishing new relationships
Avoid taking initiative, which is an important component in active dialogue	Have difficulty focusing on one conversation or person at a time

Lack spontaneity; thinking before you speak can make you come across as hesitant	Tend to talk more than you listen

Regardless of whether you're an introvert or an extrovert, you can put all your characteristics to good use as long as you have a genuine interest in other people. The abilities to be curious and interested are key when it comes to having a conversation with another person.

Accessible and sociable

A good networker is a person with whom other people want to spend time. You must be accessible and sociable, especially if you're the type who has contact with other people over the phone, at meetings, or at conferences, etc. People need to feel like they can approach you. Consider the following questions:

- Do you know if you're accessible and sociable?
- Do people find it easy to spend time with you?
- Do people think you're easy to contact?
- Do people like you the first time they meet you?

There are numerous studies showing that people remember your mood, energy levels, and ability to be interesting and interested in others. It makes them want to trade with you and recommend you to others. One study carried out by The Academy of Management Journal shows that your mood has a direct impact on your client's mood and readiness to make a purchase.

Five important qualities
All the competence and intelligence in the world won't get you anywhere if you aren't good at being around people and communicating with your surroundings. In my experience, there are five qualities that allow you to reach your goals through your network:

- You have integrity,
- People like spending time with you,
- You take responsibility in your relationships,
- Your skills are in demand, and
- You make your mark, so others remember and recognize you.

We're all different and, seeing as you must network with all sorts of people, you must keep developing as a people connoisseur, which means you should be able to succeed at the following:

- Tolerating others and maintaining strong social skills in general,
- Being inclusive and having a positive attitude toward people,
- Accepting change, and
- Understanding the world and your community.

The real hurdle is your comfort zone
When trying to sell through your relationships, you must realize that it takes time and that things don't work out sometimes. It takes a lot of energy because the whole process is about people. So many people have tremendous luck when it comes to changing their lives and occasionally going on autopilot to increase their success as networkers. If you want, you can do it, too. If you work on your desire and ability to handle change, you'll see that a once negative comfort zone can slowly turn into a positive development zone that supports and improves your ability to network with people who are different to you, as well as people who complement you.

Being a talented networker demands an immense amount of mental energy because that's what it takes to make space for other people. If you want to network, you must make room for other people. Keep the following two pieces of advice in mind:

- Be tolerant to improve your ability to be inspired by others. Don't be prejudiced.
- You have to cope with change and be curious to know where new relationships and experiences can potentially lead.

A talented networker is open-minded, tolerant, adaptable, and curious. Do you live up to those criteria? Try to pinpoint how well developed these qualities are when it comes to you specifically:

Quality	Somewhat limited	Moderately developed	Highly developed
Open-mindedness			
Tolerance			
Adaptability			
Curiosity			

360-degree analysis

If you want to develop the qualities listed above, I recommend doing a 360-degree analysis to help you figure out what you have to offer or how you can develop something to offer.

During a 360-degree analysis, you ask colleagues, clients, partners, and other people around you to talk about your strengths and the areas in which you have room for improvement (with the above qualities in mind). You can set up this analysis with the help of your closest leader.

I recommend this kind of analysis because, although it's important to know how you see yourself, it's also important to know how others see you. It's because you should change who you are according to who other people think you should be; rather you should complete this activity because it's important to know your potential and where you could benefit from further development.

Your own analysis

You can also decide to set up an analysis on your own without a leader. To do your own 360-degree analysis, you need to define the parts of yourself that you want to know more about. I recommend focusing on the four areas outlined above.

You'll need a selection of confidential and critical individuals from your network who are willing to give you this feedback. You should ask two to four people to participate and avoid involving people who know you personally, such as your partner, close friends, or family members. The people you ask for feedback should be familiar with you on a personal and a professional level, and it's important that you choose them with care.

Ensure that the people you choose to involve in the process genuinely want you to benefit from the process and that they won't just feed your words straight back to you. Every person involved needs to be capable of giving constructive and genuine feedback. They need to be qualified and representative of your surroundings.

Map out your current network

The three circles of your network

You'll find that it's a major advantage to map out your professional network so you can understand who you know and how well you know them. The act of mapping out your network takes a long time the first time around, but, once that's done, it'll be easy to update and you'll always have the overview you need.

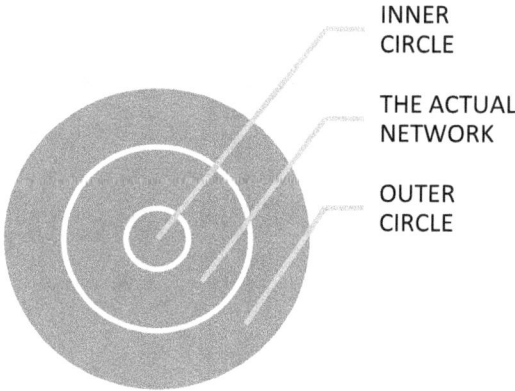

Your inner circle

Grab a piece of paper and write down the names of the people who matter most to you in terms of reaching your target turnover. Your inner circle typically consists of ten to twelve clients, and you should take great care when pinpointing them. By including them in your inner circle, you're saying that these are the people to whom you're happy to dedicate more than sixty percent of your networking time.

You can't have people you don't know yet in your inner circle, but you can have a plan for who you eventually want to have in your inner circle. Once you've written their names down, you need to recruit them and build a relationship that will eventually land them in the most important part of your network. Your inner circle develops alongside you and your goals, which means that the people you need in your inner circle may change as time passes.

The actual network
The actual network consists of people you can call who will not only recognize your name but also will want to call you back if you leave them a message asking them to do so. Your relationship with the clients in your network isn't as confidential as your relationship with those in your inner circle. There are usually around fifty clients in the actual network. These relationships are important, albeit not as important as the ones in your inner circle. The actual network consists of the people you would classify as acquaintances.

Your outer circle:
Your outer circle consists of a whole bunch of people. There can be hundreds of people in your outer circle. These are the people you meet at social and professional gatherings or the people with whom your client has a relationship. You might only know their first names and you likely don't know all that much about them. The reason you should map out this circle is that it can serve as inspiration when deciding which relationships to nourish, thereby moving people into your actual network or potentially even your inner circle.

You can map your outer circle by going through your business card organizer in chronological order. Look through address books, business card holders, contact lists, old emails, LinkedIn, Facebook, Twitter, and any other places where you have contacts. Get all your contacts organized in the same place to give you an overview of your outer circle. Some people prefer to start with this circle before moving names into the other two circles.

While mapping out your network, you might realize that you spend time on people you shouldn't be spending a lot of time on because they don't have a strategic function that benefits your business or your general direction. You might also realize that you're regularly overlooking important relationships to whom you really should be dedicating more time.

Expand your network

How to be memorable

You might find yourself in a situation where you must update your network with new clients and contacts that you need to know but haven't met yet. When that happens, it's important to have a look at where you can meet the people you're missing.

To achieve your commercial goals, you have to get out and recruit these people. Once that's done, you have to use your existing network to figure out if you know anyone who knows anyone who knows the people in question. If it turns out that you don't, think about what other avenues you could pursue to meet these people. Don't be afraid to build relationships with people of different ages, industrial affiliations, and educational backgrounds than yourself. These relationships will only strengthen your ability to solve problems. Reach out to people through your existing network through emails, direct phone calls, and social media. Tell the people you meet that you're working toward an introduction to and a relationship with X or Y.

Ask for advice from people you know for contacting these individuals. You'll be surprised by how happy people are to help you. Do you have the option to seek out one or more of the people on your list through conferences or their local lectures? Can you comment on blog posts, articles, or other things they've written? You must be creative when it comes to expanding your network.

When you meet these important contacts
Some day in the future, you'll find yourself standing in front of one or more of the people with whom you want to build a relationship. Knowing that you'll be in this position at some point, it's important to consider what you want to say to them when you finally cross paths. Think about why the individual in question needs to meet with you or talk to you. Why should they use their precious time on you? I recommend writing down three to five questions that you want to ask the person, along with considering an explanation as to why they should dedicate some of their time to being in your company.

The first networking session
At some point, you'll be invited to the highly anticipated meeting. How will you make a good impression? Start by following these tips:

- Present yourself in a positive manner.
- Don't talk negatively about anyone else, regardless of how much you want to. Control yourself, even if you happen to talk about your competitors.
- Let the other people at the meeting speak.
- Ask good questions. Come prepared.
- Support the other people at the meeting to the best of your abilities. Praise your colleagues. Be a kind and safe harbor for people in this cold world. Smile when people look at you. Be approachable and be a good human being.

When you take part in a networking session, it's important to make sure that you let the other person say what they need to say while making the most of the short time you have available. You might be used to sales meetings, which are all about closing the sale. The same principle applies to networking sessions with the exception that you need to focus on building a lasting relationship with the other person. For that reason, it's essential that you build up a conversation based on the principles of networking.

Being a good networker means that you accept responsibility for your own sale, as well as for the career and general success of your new contact. Always ask, "How can I help you?"

A networking session is a dialogue. In other words, it's an exchange of verbal and physical language cues between two or more people who want to develop a relationship with one another. You take turns playing out the roles of sender and receiver in the conversation. Keeping up a conversation with a stranger when the whole thing becomes trivial is an art, in and of itself. When you have the chance to network, you need to get to know the person well enough to figure out whether you can help them and vice versa. There's more to the conversation than exchanging information and knowledge about one another; you must create and maintain a lasting relationship.

The 30-minute rule
As a rule of thumb, a conversation in which both parties get the chance to communicate their points lasts between twenty to forty-five minutes and one to two hours. We should be able to shorten that to around 30 minutes, but most of us are incapable of uncovering another person's interests in that amount of time, which is why these conversations tend to run on a little longer.

Good networking conversations consist of the following elements:

- Both parties get to speak,
- You spend just as much time asking questions as answering them,
- You're responsible for ensuring that the person with whom you're speaking understands the current and future needs that they need to know to help you,
- The conversations can be defined as a genuine attempt to reach a mutual understanding, and
- The conversation is confidential.

Triangular Conversations
A conversation is like a triangle. The three corners consist of the introduction, conclusion, and the follow-up. At the center is the information you gained.

Most of us are active in the lead-up to a meeting and the meeting, itself, but our follow-ups are negligible. Many people send out an email, thanking the other person for the meeting and passing on information, resources, etc. If you want to build a lasting relationship with someone, that's not enough. If you've uncovered the other person's interests, you'll have an insight into the person's everyday life, which will tell you what the individual is thinking about, considering, worrying about, etc. Take responsibility for the development of the relationship and for ensuring that you go from being formal and professional to informal and personal.

Successful contact with new clients

Moving from formal to information when you meet potential clients

The acts of remembering things, remembering people, buying, and selling are all about feelings. Eighty to ninety percent of the time, your clients are using their brains subconsciously, which means that their emotions control them.

Your run-of-the-mill, salaried employee has meetings and conversations with a vast range of people every single day. At work, they receive calls, emails, and invitations left and right, asking them to attend events, evenings with their clients, conferences, etc. Talk about invitation overload. Analyses indicate that we're only capable of remembering (in detail) about one-third of all the emails and meetings we receive and attend.

What are you doing to make sure that the people you talk to, write to, and call don't forget you? How are you ensuring that you don't get lost in the crowd? What are you putting in to make sure that people remember you, the company you represent, and the skill set you have to offer?

Client relationships are all about your willingness to bundle your clients, as well as your willingness to apply yourself in a relationship. They're about you and your team, the people who participate in meetings and attend conferences. They're about the chemistry you have with the people around you.

It's strange, especially considering that we know the reason people trade with one another (and the reason some clients choose not to purchase your products) has to do with whether a client likes you and your company in terms of reputation. Whether or not they like you is linked to culture and chemistry.

Clients are sensible, intelligent, critical, and busy. In fact, they're so busy that they hate wasting their time. What does that mean for you? You must be likeable without coming across as insincere. To be credible, you must mean what you say and do what you think is right. It's all about being willing to change your habits and being curious when it comes to other people and their lives. That's what makes you seem like you care. If you care about them, people will care about you.

The other day, I was with one of my close friends, a man who has been recognized as one of the most talented French thinkers of our time. He's incredibly successful, and his story is thought-provoking. As a child, he was top of the class for a full decade. He was the most talented student, but he didn't have any friends at school. He might have been smart, but he was also lonely. As a teenager, he joined an elite school because he was one of the fifty smartest people in the country. In this new, elite class of his, though, he ended up being one of the worst students.

By changing schools and accepting his new position in the hierarchy, he learned that you must find a way to compensate if you're not getting top marks. Thus, he started hosting parties, arranging trips, and setting up various social events. He became incredibly popular, and he suddenly had more friends than he could count. He eventually ended up clawing his way back to the top of the class, but he never let himself forget that a combination of academic and social intelligence is the way to the top. He concluded that there are social and political advantages to being good at making friends, but you don't make friends in a conference room.

These days, he works with some of the most powerful people in the world. His downturn pushed him toward new social skills.

Not too long ago, we were sitting in my living room and talking to my husband about how drained we were after yet another marathon week of long days and late nights on a business trip. The conversation was mainly about why we give it our all both at work and at home, and the answer wasn't difficult to uncover: because it works and it's fun. That's why I'm sitting here, thinking about how I work and structure my days and nights. I've gotten lucky as far as that's concerned. The following statements describe some fundamental things about me:

- I'm curious, which helps motivate me.
- I'm in great health and have good stamina.
- I have an understanding partner.
- I've always been a social creature (extrovert).
- I love people, food, and social activities; it's a global phenomenon, so it gets you far! ;-)
- I've always prioritized social events like dinners, receptions, dance floors, and bars. Being able to dance is a valuable skill; I'll tell you that for free. Another close friend of mine, a brilliant neuroscientist, taught

- themselves to do the tango, and now they're known for being a dancing professor.
- I learned to spot the structure of a typical power play early on. It didn't take me long to realize that not all decisions are made in a conference room; most of them are made before a meeting even takes place or later that day/night. Sticking around is always a good idea.
- I'm good at remembering to go home at a reasonable time, and I never get too drunk, which has a negative effect on your surroundings. It's incredibly unprofessional, but in some places in Asia, people appreciate the act of getting incredibly drunk together. I've recently come back from a trip to Japan, so I can confirm that to be true.
- I don't try to maintain a perfect work-life balance. As I've said, I put so much energy into the social side of things that there's not really any balance to speak of. Then again, I've never been all that interested in balance, although I do seamlessly combine work and time off.

Be curious and open

I always adapt to local traditions, whether it's shisha in the Middle East, rice wines on the Asian continent, or draft beer in Germany. I go to karaoke bars in China and Japan, hit up nightclubs in Russia, attend bonfire parties in Mongolia, and walk down red carpets all over the States. I participate in everything they plan. I don't sleep a lot when I'm on a business trip, but I never complain about jet lag or lack of sleep. I can rest at home. I show up in a good mood with a smile on my face, and I'm always prepared.

I know so many people who go to bed early, get up to run every morning, have most of their meetings in conference rooms, and never invite their business connections to their homes. They don't participate in social events at work, and they never stick around for work drinks. They never take their career to the next level. Now, that's controversial.

We host visitors from abroad multiple times a month. I pick them up at the airport and we invite them out for dinner as a family. I have a present ready, I show them around, and we always give them the offer to stay at our house. It takes up a lot of time, but it's time well spent. There are a few advantages to do so:

- You have a great time learning about new cultures and people,
- Your guests get to know you privately, which builds trust and benefits your business, and
- Your spouse gets to know your business connections and becomes more supportive of your busy schedule (read: if they get less jealous, which is an issue for some businesswomen).

Unless you're abstaining from drinking for religious/health reasons, I genuinely encourage you to have a glass of wine or champagne when it's offered.

A lot of countries have a saying that you haven't truly met someone until you've had a drink with them. I'm not telling you to party your way to a career, but it helps if you can!

How to quickly build a personal relationship: be interested and interesting

When you meet someone for the first time, you need to spend the first one to two minutes wisely. What are you talking about? Does it foster a sense of trust or is it just small talk? Here are some tips:

- Always aim to create a good dialogue because that'll make people remember you.
- Be genuinely interested and curious in every conversation you have with your clients. Ask and listen.
- Find out how you can help each other; remember to highlight your own qualities in an elegant and straightforward way so your clients or potential clients can get an overview of who you are, what you can do, and what it is that you want.

There's a better chance that people will remember you if you replace, "My title is x," with something like, "I help people x." That kind of phrasing establishes your value and helps people understand what exactly it is that you do. Be personable and personal. Tell them why you're doing what you're doing, who you are as a person outside of work, and all that sort of stuff. That's the kind of thing people remember.

Elements to the visit

This section will walk you through the different elements that need to be incorporated over the course of a visit to create and develop a strong client relationship.

1. Be personal: give them something personal to build an atmosphere of trust. If you do it right, you can build mutual trust in just five minutes.
2. Be present. Maintain eye contact and focus on the conversation you're having in the moment, rather than what you need to do afterward. People can feel it when you're not present. Evaluate your efforts. Ask the other person what you need to work on if you feel like things aren't progressing according to plan. People will appreciate your genuine interest.

From formal to informal

Put in the effort to get to know people better. Always ask good questions on three different levels to ensure that you get a rounded impression of who it is that you're talking to.

The Professional Level: Ask questions about the person's organization and/or industry. Examples of questions you could ask include the following: "What's the current state of your organization?" "What are the main challenges facing the industry?" "What steps do you think you need to take in this particular situation?" "What changes would you like to see within the next two years?" There are plenty of other excellent questions you could ask; all you must do is find them.

The Technical Level: Ask questions about the person's skills and knowledge so you know their capabilities, their desires, and their technical and professional dreams.

The Personal Level: Ask questions about their personal life. Find out what they want out of life. Make sure to ask the kinds of questions that you would want someone to ask you. Stay focused so the other person feels like you genuinely want to know more about them.

Be respectful of other people and their time. People hate people who waste their time or stand in the way of their work. Stick to your agreements, stay brief and concise, and be respectful when you talk to people. They could be busy or on their way to their next meeting.

The 70/30 rule
The 70/30 rule just means that you spend seventy percent of your time with other people talking about work-related things like the tasks and problems at hand - the professional things. You then spend the remaining thirty percent of the time talking about personal (not private) matters. Talk about the things that are on your mind and what you're considering, or the things that bug, worry, or excite you.

Make sure to ask your conversational partner about these sorts of things, as well. Remember the short, personal anecdotes people share with you and follow up on the next time you meet. Give them something personal to make sure the relationship becomes informal. Remaining professional, formal, and distant, affects the odds of building a relationship with someone and their perception of your professional ability. Their opinion of you depends on your level of personal trust.

Caring for (new) client relationships

One of the most important things in networking is caring for the relationships you already have. A healthy and well-maintained network is the perfect foundation for expansion. If you don't care for the people you already have in your network, word will get out and you'll struggle to get new connections. When you live a busy life, it's all too easy to forget to care for your relationships with your clients.

You need to have an idea of how people want to be maintained. For some people, the occasional text is enough, while others prefer to meet up for dinner every six months. When you have a relationship with a person, you need to maintain it to ensure its development.

The following circle shows an example of a year in which you make sure to care for your network:

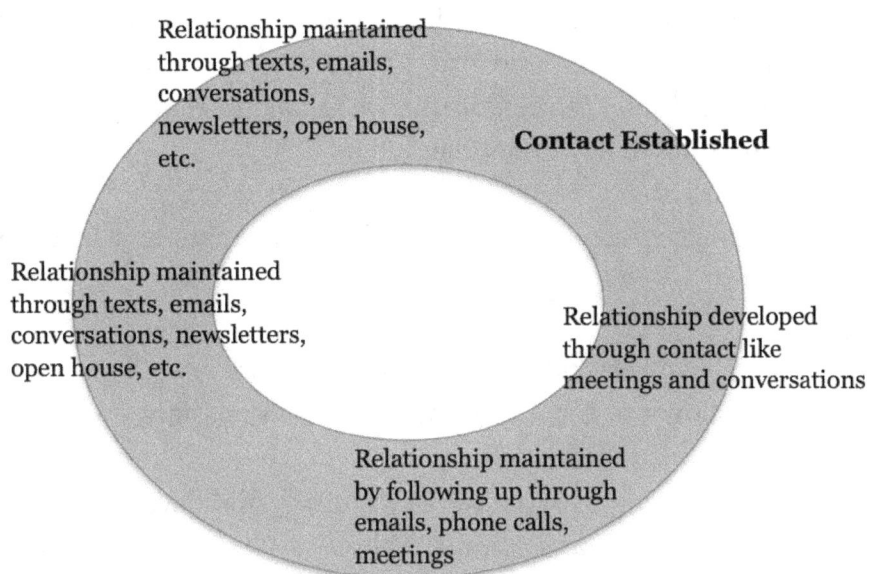

Networks are like an herb garden. You must sow the seed and water it to eventually harvest it. What I mean by that is that you need to work on caring for your relationships before you need them. If you think that sounds time-consuming, that's because it is. I don't recommend trying to network with more people than your energy allows.

A lot of people network when they desperately need something, rather than the ideal way, which is to preemptively network. You need to establish and develop relationships on a continuous basis; otherwise, they lose value. As a rule of thumb, it shouldn't take you longer than fourteen days to follow up when someone's given you their business card. Call them, email them, or write them a physical letter. Just do something to get the ball rolling.

All relationships have a set life cycle. Some relationships are meant to last forever, and others last only a couple of weeks. No matter what kind of relationship we're talking about, you must pay attention to its development.

In general, most relationships go through phases that follow a pattern:

- You meet and exchange information after which you follow up, meet, communicate, and possibly even start trading together.
- You contact each other occasionally and develop a sense of cohesion and confidentiality.
- After some time, the contact becomes informal because you feel comfortable around each other.

Whether or not you get through all the phases depends on your ability and desire to turn a formal connection into an informal one.

Most of us are good at establishing relationships, but not everyone is good at optimizing and developing relationships, along with figuring out how to make money by selling to their contacts. Many of us are good at opening the door and getting someone's contact details but turning a formal connection into an informal and mutually valuable one is nothing short of an art form.

Take your time getting to know your connections to ensure that you can give every one of them the highly individualized treatment they expect.

Make room for differences

The ways in which people want to be contacted and updated when it comes to the activities of you and your organization differ from person to person. There's nothing wrong with asking people for their preferences. Some prefer when contact is established and maintained through (frequent) physical meetings while others prefer a combination of physical meetings and virtual networking or social media. Some prefer emails, while others prefer texts. Some will trust you almost immediately, and others will take their time. The below chart is an overview of different generations and the communication methods they tend to prefer. The figure is a generalization and is meant to provide an overview to help you identify the ideal mode of contact.

Method/Generation	Baby boomers	Generation X	Generation Y	Generation Z
Physical meetings	To a large extent	In the beginning	To a small extent	Not relevant
Emails/letters	To a large extent	To some extent	To a small extent	Not relevant
Calls/texts/chats	No texting	To a large extent	To a large extent	Texts/Tweets/Messenger
Web II/social media	To a small extent	To some extent	To a large extent	Preferable

Loyal relationships (test the waters)

You know that you have a loyal relationship with a client or contact if the following points are true:

- The person always responds to your queries.
- The person forgives you for making small errors.
- The person recommends you to others.
- The person offers their critique and spends time complaining if you mess up.

If you're unsure of whether your clients are interested in you, ask yourself the following questions.

- Do they respond relatively quickly? If the answer is yes, the person at least wants to communicate.
-
- Do they respond with an affirmative answer relatively quickly (within two days) if you ask them for a meeting? Do they offer concrete suggestions for times and dates?
- Do they respect your commitments to each other and follow up to plan for the next step?
- Are you both preoccupied with getting something out of the relationship, and is there a good exchange of questions and answers? You need to have good personal chemistry and a flow to your dialogue.

As a rule of thumb, it would be reasonable to assume that if someone cancels on you two to three times, it's because they're busy. Often, though, the problem is that they aren't prioritizing you because they don't necessarily want to meet you. If someone cancels on you without suggesting an alternate date, that tends to be a clear sign that they're not all that interested, which should just motivate you to become an even more interesting person. If you're leaving three or more messages, it's time to stop. The person on the other end just isn't that into you.

Consider the following checklist for reaching out to your clients:

- Pay attention to whether your clients get back to you when you reach out to them.
- Make sure that your clients don't have any reason to complain about your leaving them messages, spamming them with emails, texting them incessantly, and taking up their time for no reason.
- Be moderately persistent. It's fine to be persistent because you want to develop a relationship with a client but be respectful about it and make sure to contact the person on the other end the way they prefer to be contacted. Every case is different. Listen to what they're saying and writing.
- People are polite, and a nice answer isn't always an invitation to continue the conversation. Read between the lines and try to figure out if the other person is genuinely interested. Don't be too formal when you talk to them. Be professional but personal, which will foster a sense of trust.

- Discuss your method of communication with your colleagues (e.g. over email). CC one of your colleagues on all communications with your client for a couple of days, then put aside some time to discuss whether you're writing emails that people want to receive and read or whether being too distant and professional. You must learn to write emails, letters, and texts, not to mention that you should be able to participate in meetings in a way that makes your clients remember you fondly.

Networking situations

There are a thousand and one ways to meet people. Many of us know to take advantage of every situation and optimize our productivity to ensure that we get as much as possible out of every meeting and conversation we have with potential clients. It might be useful to remember that when two people interact, the relationship must go through some general phases.

It's important to highlight that a relationship is carefully steered through a cycle from formality to informality that enables a connection to go from a fully professional connection to a personal professional one.

Furthermore, it's important to remember to adjust your efforts depending on whether you're talking about a physical meeting, a conference, or something like a reception. By adjusting your behavior, you ensure that you repeat the exact reward you want in the long run.

When people meet you at general meetings, receptions, or sales meetings, they size you up to evaluate their current and future relationship with you. Do they want to spend their valuable time and resources on you? Do you know what they're looking for? They measure you by the following attributes:

- Your personality as reflected by your EQ (mutual trust and chemistry),

- Your current power base (your existing network within and outside the industry),
- Your current/future skills and competences (your potential), and
- What they stand to gain from establishing a relationship with you.

Your personality needs to inspire truth; otherwise, the client won't trust your products or your organization. Clients and partners have become more critical and have started prioritizing authentic and meaningful relationships with people they can trust. Trust is the most important factor in generating sales, but it's difficult to create and easy to lose.

Your ability to build trusting and loyal relationships in a short amount of time (i.e. at a meeting) is a prerequisite for gaining access to contacts, contracts, inspiration, influence, and information. It usually takes the client about ten to thirty seconds to decide whether they trust or mistrust you, so you don't have a lot of time to make yourself look interesting. The only way to get ahead is to have a genuine interest in the client's needs and goals for the future.

The world-famous social researcher Francis Fukuyama and the equally famous Nobel Prize winner Gary Becker support the notion that the societies, leaders, and organizations that manage to establish the most trust are the ones that do best in the long run."

Relevant networking situations

The list of potential situations for relevant networking is endless, but below are some of the most obvious:

Sales meetings

Both parties are aware that the conversation will be about their businesses and potential collaboration, hence the name. A sales meeting should ideally be separate into three phases to create a solid foundation that allows the client to 1) look forward to the meeting, 2) contribute as much as possible to the meeting, and 3) remember the meeting after the fact.

Before the meeting: Who's expected to be at the meeting? Do you know the person or the people? What do you know about them (e.g. interests, age, gender, nationality, educational background)? How strong is your relationship? How long have you known each other? What do they think about your products? What's your history with the client? What's their agenda? What are their current needs and future goals (for the next one to two years)? What do your colleagues, and your team know about the participants at the meeting? Are there any articles about them? What does Google have to say?

At the meeting: During the sales meeting, it's important to follow the 70/30 rule. A good meeting is a meeting in which the dialogue is equal. Don't be too impersonal, professional, impartial, and distant. Make sure you take meetings in places other than just conference rooms. People are more likely to remember meetings of high emotional frequency (EF) than meetings that are all about technical details. How are you going to create and maintain a high EF level across all your meetings?

Follow-up meetings: It's important to follow up after a meeting, and you should do this as an extension of your physical meeting. I recommend following up after a couple of days. Whether you show up in person, write an email, call, write a text, or send an article or a book just depends on what you consider appropriate for the situation and what you agreed on during the meeting. You always must give your clients something that means something to them. This is where you get the chance to personalize gifts to ensure that they suit the individual and your relationship. Steer clear of clinical emails and voicemails. Try to establish an emotional connection with your clients. Show them how warm and compassionate you are. Be the kind of honest and interesting person with whom people want to spend time .

During and after all meetings, you should have a think about what you need to give and want to take from your relationship. A connection who experiences a sense of mutuality is more inclined to think that you have a solid relationship.

Conferences
If you're looking to maximize your impact at conferences, it helps to have the right tools and a solid game plan in place. Platforms like Brella, and Eventbrite offer features to manage schedules, facilitate networking, and coordinate meeting spaces, making it easier to stay organized and connect with the right people.

Using tools can help streamline your efforts, ensuring you have more time for meaningful conversations and less time worrying about logistics.

3 Tips to Set Up Successful Meetings Before a Conference: Start identifying key attendees and prospective contacts a few weeks in advance. Use LinkedIn or X (formerly Twitter), TikTok, LinkedIn etc. to learn about them, their interests, and recent activity. Once you've shortlisted potential contacts, reach out with a personalized message expressing your interest in meeting during the conference. Share on social media that you'll be attending the conference. This lets others know you'll be there and opens the door for connections - people may reach out to coordinate a meeting or simply say hello!

When you're specific and relevant in your approach, people are much more likely to respond.

Follow and engage. One powerful way to establish rapport ahead of time is by following people on IX. Engage with their posts, comment thoughtfully, and even share their insights if they resonate with you. For high-priority contacts, consider sending a direct message to introduce yourself and mention why you'd like to connect. By the time you meet in person, you've already built a warm connection, making that first conversation smoother and more meaningful.

Suggest a time and place - and make it convenient. When proposing a meeting, consider the flow of the conference. Suggest locations that are easy to access, like spots near the main conference area, or invite them for a quick coffee during a break. If they're pressed for time, offer to keep it short and flexible. This way, you're respecting their time and maximizing the chances of a productive meeting.

The key is to be proactive, intentional, and personable - you're not just setting up a meeting; you're building relationships.

Conferences can be a waste of time if you're (only) going to listen to the speakers and lecturers. It might be useful, intellectually speaking, but it doesn't get you anywhere as far as sales are concerned. If you have clients or partners with you, it's important to be a good host, thereby giving people a memorable experience. Being a good host isn't exactly a walk in the park. You must be comfortable with the role because it's about your surroundings, the program, and your ability to be a personable host who's both interested and interesting. Do you know how to act at conferences and other events with high attendance?

Below, I've outlined some archetypes of people who attend conferences. Try to find the one that best describes you:

The Neutral Opener: You tend to talk about neutral topics while you circle the food or wait to greet the host. You prefer to play it safe and tend to hover around the food, the gifts, the bathrooms, and the group of people congratulating the host for this, that, and the next thing. You don't talk a lot and when you do, it's usually just to the people you happen to be standing or sitting next to. You're polite and distant. You love bumping into people you know because they put you back in your comfort zone. You try not to rouse attention, and you like hovering around natural meeting points. You don't ask people for their business cards. You leave it up to other people to initiate conversations.

Tips for the neutral opener:

It's easy to be a person to whom people don't remember talking because you didn't tell them anything personal. Practice describing yourself in a short and interesting way that makes people remember and like you. Try to write out three to five routine questions to ask people you don't know. Practice keeping up good networking dialogue. Practice taking initiative and being more proactive. Walk around instead of standing still. Say hello to people you don't know and realize that it isn't all that dangerous after all. Remember to smile, as simple as that advice is. When you show people that you're happy to be there, you make it that much easier for them to like you.

The Follower: Many of us are followers when we find ourselves in big groups of people where it's up to us to seek out certain people and situations. Followers tend to gravitate toward groups of people they know or don't know yet. To them, the most important thing is to avoid too much attention. Does that sound like you? If so, chances are that you discreetly infiltrate groups of people without ever actually talking that much. In other words, you sneak your way into the group. You stand where other people are already standing.

Tips for the follower:
Let people know that you're joining the group. When they inevitably look up at you, take advantage of the moment and say hello to everyone. Make sure your voice is open and welcoming to ensure that everyone pays attention to you when you speak. If there are multiple people participating in the conversation, say hello to each of them in turn. Remember to smile; that leaves a positive first impression! Studies show that we like people whose behavior resembles our own because we see ourselves in them.

That's a tool you need to learn. Listen to what other people are saying and keep the ball rolling, so you eventually get around to telling them who you are and why you're there.

The Attention-Seeker: You're the person who is either offered or commands attention. You tend to laugh and speak a little louder than everyone else, and people gravitate toward you. You love attention and navigate formal and informal relationships effortlessly. You always stand where everyone can see you.

Tips for the attention seeker:
Make sure to give other people the chance to speak. Ask the people on the sidelines looking in to join you. Leave people with the impression that you're curious and attentive by maintaining eye contact and letting others finish their sentences. Give other people the chance to speak and shine. You don't need all the attention for yourself. It's great to be funny and to have people gravitate toward you, but the trick is using your ability to be the life of the party to lift other people up. That'll leave them with a positive impression of you.

The Need Networker: You're not particularly elegant, and you're not interested in wasting time. Your goal is to gather as many business cards as humanly possible. You have your elevator pitch ready to go and you actively scan the room with the intention of getting as much as possible out of as many people as possible as quickly as possible. You stand where you have a good view of the room.

Tips for the need networker:

You might come across as overly goal oriented. People attend events because they want to be seen, meet new people, and work on the relationships they already have. It's generally frowned-upon to show up for the sole purpose of networking. Read the room and the people to whom you speak. Do they want to network, or are they there because they want to talk to you for a second before moving on for good? Work on reading people so you don't misread the needs of yourself and others.

You don't need to talk to a lot of people, but it's important to have an in-depth conversation with the people you do talk to. Quality over quantity.

The Busy Bee: You hate attending receptions and conferences and the main reason you show up is to please your employer or the host. You rush to the event, drop off your present, grab a snack, and leave. You talk briefly to a few people without exchanging business cards. You don't have time to stand anywhere in particular because you're practically out the door before you've even arrived.

Tips for the busy bee:
Be present (even if you only have two minutes). Just because a conversation is short doesn't have to mean it's forgettable. It all depends on what you're like during those two minutes.

Regardless of which type of networker you are, it's important that you start enjoying, or at least appreciating, situations where you encounter strangers. If you're nervous, it might help to know who's coming, so reach out to the host in advance and ask them to introduce you to X, Y, or Z. You need to prepare yourself for the event before you arrive. You know people are going to ask you about certain things, so you should take your time to prepare your response for when people inevitably ask you about your job, the future, etc. By prepping questions to ask the others in advance, it'll be easier to focus on enjoying the event than it would be if you had to juggle enjoying the event with thinking of good questions.

If you find yourself at a conference without your clients, you should think about who you want to meet and how you want to meet them. What interesting people can you meet at the conference? At most conferences, you'll find that the speakers aren't hiding in the VIP section; rather, they're mingling with the participants and attending each other's presentations to ask intelligent questions. Use this time to reach out to them; they'll find it exciting.

Set aside time to socialize and find yourself some good connections. Start debating an issue by drawing on all the different people, opinions, and experiences in the room. These days, a lot of people are on Twitter, and I often tweet at people to tell them that I can't wait to hear from them/meet them. Even the busiest people love when you tweet at them. You could even ask the host of the event to introduce you.

The following bullet points are a list of questions to consider before attending a conference:

- Who's coming? Ask for the attendance sheet.
- Are you arriving as a group, or are you arriving alone?

- What role do you need to play to get as much positive contact with the participants as possible (if you're the one hosting the conference)?

When you're at the conference, there's an extra list of questions to consider, as well:

- Get an overview of speakers and workshops. Which events do you want to attend?
- Can you get a moment with some of the speakers?
- Can you invite a VIP person from the conference to introduce to your client?
- Which studies are going to be covered at the conference? Are you there in the capacity of a sponsor, speaker, or co-host? What are your responsibilities?
- Have you planned for client/networking meetings, receptions, etc.?
- Where are people staying? Are you staying at the same hotel as someone with whom you want to establish a relationship?
- Have you planned activities for every night or is it possible to take the initiative on that front and invite people to join you?

Finally, when the conference is over, you're still not quite done with reflections and checklists. Consider the following questions:

- Have you agreed to follow up on the people you exchanged business cards /scanned WhatsApp or LinkedIn profiles with?
- Is there anything you need to find out or have promised to get back to them about?
- Can you take the next step and ask to set up a call or meeting?

Business Dinners

Over the years, I've attended more than 500 business dinners across 50+ countries, each with its own local traditions and customs. One of the most crucial lessons I've learned is to always do your homework - understanding and respecting cultural norms is essential. A simple misstep, like using the wrong greeting or gesture, can unintentionally offend. Proper research goes a long way in building rapport and showing genuine respect for your hosts and fellow guests

Whether you're attending as a guest or hosting, business dinners offer a valuable opportunity to strengthen relationships, gather insights, and showcase your professionalism.

Here are some key questions and considerations to maximize the impact of your dinner engagement.

Before the Dinner:
1. *Research the Attendees.* Know who will be attending and, if possible, study their backgrounds and current roles. This helps you identify shared interests or relevant business points. If anyone from your organization has

history or ongoing discussions with certain attendees, be aware of those connections.

2. *Understand the Seating Arrangement.* If you have any say in the seating plan, consider positioning yourself strategically. This could mean sitting near key decision-makers, stakeholders, or clients you're looking to build rapport with. If you're not organizing the dinner, try to get a look at the seating arrangement in advance to plan your interactions.

3. *Prepare Topics of Conversation.* Think ahead about neutral yet engaging topics that suit the interests and roles of each participant. Steer clear of polarizing issues that may create tension (like certain political topics). Instead, focus on industry trends, common business challenges, and achievements. Keeping the conversation inclusive and insightful can set a positive tone and help build connections.

4. *Be Mindful of Timing and Discretion.* Business dinners often blend formal and informal tones, so it's important to read the room. If sensitive discussions arise, be prepared to shift topics gracefully and maintain a discreet tone. Your attire should also match the setting - dressing well but not overly formal helps you come across as approachable and adaptable.

5. *Set Personal Goals:* Define what you aim to accomplish during the dinner. Is it a chance to nurture a potential client relationship, align on project goals, or simply gain insights from an industry peer? Having clear objectives allows you to make the most of the evening without pushing too hard.

6. *Follow Up.* After the event, follow up with a polite thank-you message or email to reinforce any connections you made or insights you discussed. This simple gesture demonstrates professionalism and can open doors to further conversations.

By preparing thoughtfully and staying adaptable, business dinners can be a powerful tool for relationship-building and advancing your goals, helping you to leave a lasting, positive impression.

E-mails:
After a conference, many of us rely on emails to stay connected - they're still the most widely used form of communication. However, the volume of emails people receive daily makes it difficult for any single message to stand out. Writing an engaging, memorable email can be challenging, but mastering this skill can make a significant impact.

Here's an example of the typical emails we see after conferences:

Dear [Name],

Thank you for meeting with me on [Date]. During the meeting, we discussed [Topic]. I'll follow up with more information as soon as possible.

Best regards,
[Your Name]

Dear [Name],

I'd like to arrange a meeting on [Date]. Please find the proposed agenda attached.

Best regards,
[Your Name]

Sound familiar? These types of emails often fall flat because they lack engagement. Here's why:

- The introduction lacks personalization. Generic openings don't create a meaningful connection with the recipient. There's nothing that says, "This is for you," or "This matters."
- The message is too brief. While emails should be concise, they shouldn't feel impersonal or rushed. A few extra details can make a big difference in establishing rapport.
- There's no clear call to action. If there's no specific reason to respond immediately, the email risks being forgotten.

Making Your Emails Stand Out with the **PRAC Method**
When writing emails (or letters), keep the PRAC method in mind to ensure your message is memorable and actionable:

- **P** = Personal: Tailor the message with specific references or details unique to the recipient.
- **R** = Relevant: Make the content relevant to their interests or concerns.
- **A** = Action: Include a clear, direct request or call to action.
- **C** = Contact: Make it easy for them to respond or reach you.

Avoid generic emails that start with "Dear Client" or lack any reference to the individual. People tend to ignore mass emails, and generic messages won't create the connection you need.

Personalization in Practice: A Sample Email
Imagine reaching out to someone you haven't spoken to in a while. Here's an example of how a thoughtful, personalized message can help rekindle a connection:

Dear Michael,
How are you? It's been a while! How's everything going at home and work? And how are the kids? Did you get into the school you wanted for them? We're starting the school search for our little one now, too - it's such an exciting time!

I'll be honest, Michael. I've been meaning to reconnect, but work and family life kept me busy. We have three kids now, so my focus has been all on them!

Since we last spoke, I was promoted - I'm now in charge of ensuring our key clients have access to round-the-clock resources on medical data and side effects. It's an interesting service we're currently testing in the European market, and I'd love your thoughts on it.

I'd like to reconnect with some trusted business partners to get honest feedback, and you're one of the people I value most. Would you be open to a chat? Let's catch up, and I'd love to hear how you've been, too.

Warm regards,
[Your Name]

Tips for Crafting Engaging Emails

- Start with a shared connection: Remind them of how you know each other or mention a fond memory. This creates warmth and instantly personalizes the message.
- Show appreciation: Thank them for something specific, whether it's a previous collaboration or a piece of advice they gave you.
- Be clear and direct: Once you've re-established the connection, explain why you're reaching out in a concise way. Avoid vague phrases like, "If you know anyone interested..." Instead, be specific about how they can help.
- Finish with an actionable invitation: Ask them to meet for coffee, give you a call, or connect in some other way. A clear invitation makes it easy for them to respond.

Personalizing emails may take a bit more effort, but the results are worth it. A thoughtful message shows respect, builds rapport, and keeps your contacts genuinely interested in staying connected.

Calls, Texts, and Chats: The Power of Personal Connection

In an age dominated by digital communication, a simple phone call has become an undervalued tool for building relationships. Calling someone - rather than just shooting off an email - shows initiative and allows you to convey warmth, sincerity, and intent in a way that words on a screen simply can't capture.

Next time you're about to write an email, pause and consider dialing instead. The impact of hearing your voice can transform a transactional interaction into a memorable exchange. If they don't pick up, leave a concise, thoughtful message. Keep it under a minute, be specific, and smile as you speak - tone matters more than you might think.

A brief, personal message can spark curiosity and make you the kind of person people look forward to calling back. Embracing this approach creates more meaningful connections, turning every touchpoint into an opportunity to deepen trust and rapport.

To be honest, I've seen people struggle with making effective, professional calls. Some simply say, "Please call back" - without giving any reason. Others call when they're bored, out running, or otherwise distracted, which doesn't exactly come across as professional. Always remember that the person on the other end has a busy life, full of their own responsibilities and demands. The goal is to make their life easier, not add to the complexity. Be intentional, respectful of their time, and clear about why you're reaching out.

Social Media
Whether we embrace it or resist it, social media has woven itself deeply into our personal and professional lives. Platforms like TikTok, Instagram, Discord, and X are now hubs for information sharing, dialogue, and connection. Social media is:

- A space for learning and knowledge-sharing.
- A way to share everything from files and ideas to concerns, passions, and moments of joy across personal and professional spheres.
- A dynamic forum where we engage in conversation - with friends, family, clients, employees, and investors.
- A window into someone else's world, where active participation is the bridge to understanding.

For organizations, social media offers transformative opportunities to reach audiences, build trust, and foster collaboration. Used strategically, it becomes a tool for marketing, loyalty-building, and cultivating meaningful networks.

A Few Principles for Building Connections on Social Media

1. Be authentic - but be the best version of yourself. Your voice is your brand; make it genuine, but intentional.
2. Prioritize quality over quantity. Network thoughtfully. Be strategic and selective with connections, nurturing relationships that add value for both sides.
3. Ask the Five W's. Who, What, Where, When, and Why are powerful tools for prompting others to share what's meaningful to them.
4. Clarify your own needs. Make it easy for others to understand how they can help or support you, increasing the likelihood of genuine, productive engagement.
5. Express gratitude. A simple thank-you goes a long way in fostering goodwill and reinforcing connections.

6. Be generous with your support. Helping others builds loyalty and makes people more likely to return the favor.
7. Respectfully say no when needed. If you can't assist, offer alternatives or recommendations. This keeps the relationship positive and helpful.
8. Build trust through consistency. When people feel they can rely on you, they'll be more open to sharing and collaborating.
9. Prepare before engaging. Before online events or interactions, ensure you're focused and clear on your objectives, respecting both time and resources.
10. Create a welcoming atmosphere. Social media is a conversation - help people feel comfortable, valued, and motivated to keep connecting.

In the digital age, social media isn't just a tool; it's a vibrant arena for real-world connection and opportunity. Approach it with thoughtfulness, authenticity, and strategy, and you'll find it becomes an invaluable part of your network-building toolkit.

The To-Do List
Finally, I've included a to-do list here. I wholeheartedly recommend working out a concrete plan of action for networking:

- Have you mapped out your network? Do you have the overview necessary to network in a professional and goal-oriented manner?
- Do you need to expand your network? Where can you meet people that you don't know yet (situations, events, etc.)?

- Do you need to work on maintaining some of the relationships in your network? What maintenance are you going to do to ensure that your relationships remain positive and loyal?
- Is there anything you need to work on to become the best version of yourself?

Sales and Marketing in the Year 2030

Let's face it: the lines between sales and marketing have blurred, merging into a holistic experience where relationships and reputation reign supreme. In today's world, everyone is selling something - be it a product, an idea, or a vision of the future. Our language - terms like "clients," "campaigns," "front office" - may soon seem as outdated as door-to-door sales. If you're still operating with these concepts, it's time to think much bigger.

In a world that rapidly oscillates between crisis and opportunity, motivations have evolved. Consumers are more discerning, more intentional, and more conscious of not only what they buy but also why they buy and who they're buying from. Status has shifted: it's less about accumulation and more about adding value to one's community and the world. Today's markers of influence are purpose-driven, with a focus on mental well-being, authenticity, and societal impact. The companies thriving in 2030 will be those that don't just acknowledge this shift but integrate it into their very core.

The Traditional Sales Model is Fading Fast
Outdated models, like the hunter and farmer archetypes, segmented office hierarchies, and print-driven campaigns, are nearing extinction. We're stepping into an era where agility, digital fluency, and an unwavering commitment to personalization will define the most effective sales teams. Technology will be essential, but only as a tool to deepen human

connection - enabling experiences that are authentic and customer-centered.

Consumer Behavior Has Evolved - And It's Not Reversing

Over recent years, consumption patterns have undergone a seismic shift, bringing sustainability and social impact to the forefront. Modern consumers demand quality and alignment with their values. They're asking, "What does this brand do for me?" and "What does this brand stand for?" Studies show that 63% of Gen Z and Gen Alpha`s buyers prefer brands with transparent environmental practices, while nearly 80% are loyal to companies that embrace inclusivity and sustainability. In rethinking their values, consumers are reshaping the entire market landscape.

One generation we don't talk enough about is Gen Alpha. These kids are born from 2010 to 2025, are poised to become the largest and most diverse generation in history. Approximately 2.5 million Gen Alphas are born globally each week, with projections estimating their total population to reach nearly 2 billion by 2025. In the United States, Generation Alpha is the most racially and ethnically diverse generation to date, with 47% identifying as non-white.

Education: Predictions indicate that 90% of Gen Alphas will earn a high school diploma, and 50% are expected to obtain a university degree, making them the most educated generation thus far.

Technology Integration: Raised in a digital era, Gen Alphas are highly tech-savvy, with 72% of students globally using digital devices in the classroom

Generation Alpha, often referred to as the "Sephora Generation," has been significantly influenced by the COVID-19 pandemic, which introduced unique social challenges during their formative years. The necessity of remote interactions and limited in-person socialization accelerated their digital fluency, making them more tech-savvy than any previous generation. This cohort's deep engagement with technology has also led to early and enthusiastic participation in beauty and skincare trends, with many tweens and teens actively exploring high-end products and routines.

Their adeptness with digital platforms has facilitated this engagement, as they seamlessly navigate online spaces to discover and share beauty content. This combination of heightened digital proficiency and early interest in personal care underscores Generation Alpha's distinctive consumer behaviors and preferences. By 2029, Generation Alpha's economic influence is projected to exceed $8.2 trillion, underscoring their significant role in future markets. You WILL have to deal with this generation so it's better to start studying them.

10 Trends shaping 2030 and 5 strategies for client-centered success

This chapter delves into ten transformative trends reshaping sales and marketing, complemented by five actionable strategies to position your company as an authentic, client-centered force by 2030. This new era of sales is about more than hitting targets - it's about creating a dialogue that fosters enduring trust, with transparency, credibility, and mutual respect at its core.

Today, status is marked by a bike and / or Tesla in the driveway, a local farm box on the kitchen counter, pre-loved clothes in the closet, and a public transportation pass in hand. Gone are the days of blind consumption; today's consumer is informed, intentional, and holds brands to a high standard.

The brands that thrive in 2030 will be those that embrace authenticity as their guiding principle, turning every sale into an opportunity to build trust and every product into a symbol of shared values. With consumer expectations higher than ever, the winners will be the brands that innovate fearlessly, adapt swiftly, and meet their customers in this evolving landscape - one where dialogue, transparency, and purpose define success.

Trend #1: The Era of Non-Use
As we approach 2030, a significant shift in consumer behavior is emerging: a deliberate move away from excessive consumption. This "non-use" trend reflects a growing desire for

sustainability and mindfulness in purchasing decisions. A 2023 Nielsen report indicates that 55% of global consumers are actively reducing their consumption to support environmental and personal well-being goals.

Communities like the *Buy Nothing Project* have gained momentum, encouraging individuals to share goods locally, thereby minimizing waste and fostering community connections. Platforms such as Rent the Runway and Turo exemplify this shift by enabling users to rent clothing and vehicles, respectively, promoting access over ownership.

Insight for Companies: To thrive in this environment, businesses must pivot from traditional sales tactics to strategies that emphasize intentionality and sustainability. Brands like Patagonia have successfully adopted this approach, focusing on product longevity and environmental responsibility, thereby resonating with conscientious consumers.

Trend #2: The Rise of Non-Marketing
Consumers are increasingly resistant to traditional advertising, favoring authentic, value-driven interactions. A 2024 Accenture survey found that 74% of customers are frustrated by irrelevant ads and prefer brands that engage in meaningful, personalized experiences.

In both B2B and B2C sectors, clients are gravitating toward interactive, high-value content. Forbes reports that Gen Z anticipates a 50% reduction in TV ads by 2028, with nearly 80% expecting personalized digital experiences. Companies like Glossier have capitalized on this trend by building strong communities through user-generated content and grassroots marketing, fostering loyalty without relying on traditional advertising.

Insight for Companies: To remain competitive, businesses should focus on building communities of loyal brand advocates. Empowering employees to act as brand ambassadors and engaging clients through authentic interactions can drive organic growth and deepen customer relationships.

Trend #3: Value-Living as a Brand Imperative
Consumers now demand that brands authentically embody their stated values. Edelman's 2024 Trust Barometer reveals that 86% of consumers believe CEOs should speak out on societal issues, with 72% willing to abandon brands that don't align with their ethics.

Companies like Allbirds have embraced this expectation by committing to sustainable practices and transparency in their supply chains, resonating with environmentally conscious consumers.

Insight for Companies: Brands must prioritize authenticity and ensure that every action reflects their stated values. Transparency and purpose can serve as competitive advantages, as clients increasingly seek brands that align with their personal ethics.

Action Plan for the Future of Sales and Marketing (2030)

1. Integrate Sales and Marketing: Dissolve silos between sales and marketing to create cohesive, value-driven customer engagements.
2. Hire emotionally intelligent sales professionals across all roles, including front and back office. Ensure that the most skilled individuals engage directly with consumers.
3. Build Authentic Brand Ambassadors: Equip employees to embody the brand's values, ensuring all customer interactions reflect the company's mission.
4. Leverage Technology for Trust: Utilize AI and machine learning to deliver personalized, purpose-driven content that aligns with clients' values.
5. Foster Grassroots Communities: Develop networks of loyal customers who act as brand advocates, providing organic growth and authentic endorsements.
6. Demonstrate Tangible Values: Show concrete evidence of the brand's commitments, as consumers increasingly demand visible actions that demonstrate environmental, social, and governance (ESG) commitments.

The future of sales and marketing is defined by authenticity, sustainability, and community engagement. Companies that lead will successfully merge value-living with grassroots marketing, creating meaningful connections based on shared purpose. By 2030, thriving companies will be those that prove to clients they are more than profit-driven entities, keeping pace with evolving consumer values.

Trend #4: Less But Better

Clients are no longer on the lookout for bigger, shinier, pricier products anymore. Instead, they acquire new-to-them things through considerate consumption that tends to be green, organic, borrowed, used, second-hand, rented, or at least durable. Clients are asking for less but better consumption. They want their purchases to have a purpose (no more stuff). People want responsible products. The product's raison d'être is becoming increasingly important, as having a raison d'être helps justify its existence. An organization can boost its raison d'être and thereby justify its existence by establishing a visible CSR or CSI profile (sustainability).

Trend #5: Emotional Punch

Credibility and loyalty are the byproducts of persistent, emotional impressions. If an organization wants to have any hope of getting through to its target audience, it needs to operate within three dimensions:

- Impression: the first thing they experience when coming across the organization,
- Imprint: what the client has or knows after having met you and your organization, and
- Expression: the things people say about the organization, which should ideally be consistent across the client base.

In short, corporate branding and personal branding have joined forces and, to succeed, your brand needs to be all about emotions. All employees have a personal brand or image that needs to match up with that of the organization and vice versa. The London Business School researched into client behavior and supports the notion that emotions are fifty percent of the reason we make or don't make purchases. The London Business School claims that there are twenty emotions that control or destroy our perception and desire to buy something from a particular organization. That is to say that there's a direct link between the ability of an organization to construct emotional connections and its ability to earn money. In conclusion, clients and consumers don't just shop with their heads and their wallets but they also shop with their hearts.

This emotional pull is why organizations need to hire memorable people. They need to be able to create and maintain warm relationships with their clients. It's no longer enough for a business to have the professional ability that used to help them survive. They also need to interact positively with their clients to stimulate their emotions.

The ability of the organization to establish an emotional connection with their clients is called their emotional quotient. If you want to achieve success, seek out inspiration for bundling clients. It might be a good idea to have a look at how other industries do this, so you avoid recycling old knowledge. A lot of companies have a low emotional quotient because they fail to acknowledge that success is no longer about professional ability, price, or accessibility. Those things just help you get your foot in the door. The modern weapon in the fight for people's money is the collective ability of the company to leave a positive, authentic, and emotional imprint.

All companies work in the three dimensions mentioned earlier, but they don't often know how their customers react to them or whether they're using these dimensions correctly. It's important for the organization to establish an overview of what it's doing well and where it stands to improve. If you want to lose fewer clients to your competitors, even if these competitors happen to be cheaper, you need to make sure that your organization revolves around your clients and that all employees are cast to fit your client base, not the other way around. Now, a lot of established companies think they're perceived to be successful when the reality is that people have started to say the opposite.

Trend #6: "To Give" Is the New "To Receive"
If you don't want to be the kind of organization that consumers warn each other about, you should learn to give, rather than taking. Educate all your employees to put the stakeholder before the shareholder. It's all about giving value before taking value (in the form of money) from the client. Give your clients your experience, time, and knowledge and make them feel included when it comes to your organization and your key issues. You can no longer buy clients with expensive dinners, rides in luxurious cars, or nice holidays. You can still get a long way with VIP events, but you need to adapt the nature of these events. Make sure your clients are involved in your green efforts. Skip the traditional business lunch and invite your clients out to collect trash in a park instead. Give them something that'll help them grow.

Cultivate credibility, transparency, community, and involvement. Remember that you can't take anything from your clients before you're in their good books. Give first and receive later. Stop viewing your clients as clients. Learn to consider them as employees, colleagues, members, or something similar that highlights that they are part of us, not them.

Trend # 7: "No New Customers" Strategy
This trend is all about focusing on existing clients rather than new clients (unless we're talking about a start-up in the early stages). That's why terms like hunter - a seller who specializes in finding new clients, rather than retaining existing clients - is on its way out. The most important thing these days is to retain and care for existing clients. You may execute a "no new customers" strategy by performing the following actions:

- Service and care for existing clients only, which does not include setting up any activities geared toward attracting new clients.
- Organize activities intended to create satisfied, loyal customers.
- Reward employees for achievements related to the clients, their experiences, and their perceived satisfaction.
- Reward clients for being loyal.
- Reward clients for recommending you to others.
- Manage critical clients who are dissatisfied for whatever reason.
- Find the clients who don't complain but just leave instead.

Scoring highly on client satisfaction isn't important. In fact, it can mean that you're not challenging your clients and helping them develop (read: they stay in their comfort zones). What you should aim for instead are loyal clients. Clients become loyal the moment they feel like an organization treats them positively. Other things that foster loyalty are a strong, collective corporate brand and good reviews/feedback. A client becomes loyal to your organization only if they feel as though they have direct contact with you and your employees. They want to be able to blog, send messages and emails, or call and get an answer immediately.

Loyal customers feel seen. They want to be asked why they buy or don't buy certain things. Just think about all the times you've walked out of a store without having bought anything, even though you went in there fully intending to make a purchase. The reason might have been something as simple as not being able to find your size or not finding anything in the color you wanted. It might be that there was no price tag on the chair you had your eye on or that there was no lipstick without dye. A lot of the time, it's easy to be accommodating and turn the situation around to create a sale when a client chooses not to buy something. You just can't do it if you never ask for feedback.

Trend #8: Slow Sales

Terms like marketing, front office staff, and sellers are on their way out. If the sole purpose of a term is to create a connection between different departments or to create sales, it's time for the term to go. These kinds of terms limit accessibility because they ensure that there's only one entry point for the client to use. Customer-facing job descriptions need to be upgraded to ensure that new employees create value and act as sparring partners for all clients. On top of that, organizations need to develop the will to let different relationships develop, which is a pursuit that requires more than a focus on transactions and the commercial side of things.

It might help to look at the situation in terms of fast and slow food. Fast food could be compared to fast sales. They feed you, but you don't stay full for long. Before you know it, you must go back out and find new clients in order to stay full. Clients don't tend to come back and if they do, they don't recommend your products to other people. If you look at slow food, though, you'll see that quality is the utmost priority. Rather than focusing on only consumption, slow food and slow sales focus on the entire production process.

When it comes to slow sales, you give yourself plenty of time to get to know your clients to provide personalized treatment that meets the expectations of the individual. Slow sales don't require massive marketing budgets. With a slow sales strategy, there's no interest in mass marketing campaigns because that signals that the organization wants clients to contact them and not the other way around. Massive campaigns indicate that the entire organization is waiting by the phones, ready to take orders. You turn yourself into an order-managing machine, rather than an actor ensuring client involvement.

A lot of organizations consider marketing efforts to be a way to stimulate and create an influx of new clients, but the fact of the matter is that new clients aren't that attractive. If you've earned it, existing clients will make sure to bring in new ones through their recommendations. In the future, this strategy will be the single most effective way to build and maintain a strong position in the market. It's more important at this moment than ever before.

Loyal clients confirm their purchases through net talk. People share certain messages through online environments like Facebook and Twitter, just to mention some of the biggest platforms. It's incredibly interesting that companies refuse to provide access to these social networks, or environments as I prefer to call them, seeing as a social network is something completely different. Companies refuse access to these environments during office hours when it might be beneficial to think about how employees can actively use these to improve branding. It's also important to remember that these environments are currently first-generation platforms. They're going to develop significantly and become an integrated part of how we work, think, share knowledge, market ourselves, and ensure development.

Do you and your organization have loyal clients? Most of us don't know how loyal our clients really are. We might have a low client turnover (i.e. the number of existing clients who choose to leave), but that doesn't mean that our clients are loyal. They might just be waiting to see if there is or will be an alternative to your services. You can tell your clients are loyal if they:

- Forgive you for small mistakes,
- Stay when the same service is available cheaper elsewhere,
- Recommend you to others,
- Come back for your products time and time again, and

- Offer critique and take the time to complain.

Trend #9: Direct Dialogue on Demand

An honest CEO of a sizable corporation recently told me that they don't like their clients. They told me that their employees are experts in their field and find that the clients are inferior and annoying. Many of them have expressed that they think the clients ask a bunch of "stupid questions." That's dangerous territory. You need to charm your clients every single day, and no matter how much of a nobody somebody looks like, every client matters. On average, every client knows 250 people. Whether they recommend you to these people or warn them about you is up to you.

Thanks to technology in the modern era, your clients are only a click away from destroying your reputation. Overnight, you can go from having an excellent reputation to being the kind of organization the people avoid at all costs. Your clients can easily post status updates on Facebook that reach thousands of people.

It's never been easier to share your opinion with a lot of people in a short amount of time. The client's opinion should be shared directly with the company, but that's rarely what happens. There aren't a lot of companies out there that offer a client-oriented and client-friendly channel for criticism. It's rare that a client can get in direct contact with an organization. Direct dialogue on-demand means that the organization should establish different channels to allow their clients to share their emotional frustrations. An angry client can't and won't wait until tomorrow when your reception or customer helpline is open.

If you don't have a metaphorical wall for your frustrated clients to write on or a phone number they can text angrily, you can rest assured they will blog about you for their entire social circle to see. That's not going to work out to your benefit. One of the easiest ways to decrease the likelihood of this happening is to offer an around-the-clock solution that makes sure your clients can get in touch with you at all hours. Is it expensive? Yes, but prospective clients do the most research when the product or service in question is of high economic interest or revolves around status.

Blog posts and status updates will never disappear once they're shared in cyberspace. Sure, you might get them removed, but it'll be hard work and cost you a lot of money. It's better to avoid negative publicity online in the first place because it affects whether other people want to work with you as a supplier. From a client perspective, life is too short to live every single experience, so the busier someone is, the more they'll rely on other people's recommendations. A consumer's opinion of a product is more credible than an expert's opinion.

If you come across a dissatisfied customer, keep in mind that it's good business to manage dissatisfaction effectively. If you follow-up with a caring attitude, angry or dissatisfied clients may turn into loyal clients. Sales are like marriages. The client doesn't feel that they have a solid marriage with you until there's been a conflict that you've managed to resolve. An organization shows its true self when things aren't going as planned. Check how satisfied your clients are every time they trade with you. Ask them these 5 concise questions:

- Are you satisfied?
- How satisfied are you?
- Would you recommend us to others?
- To whom would you recommend us?
- How can we improve?

In the future, clients are going to want to see that other people are satisfied with you and your organization, so feel free to share your satisfaction and loyalty scores. You might not be the top of the list but being aware of and transparent with your value shows that you're committed to combating dissatisfaction. Get your clients involved. Invest time in establishing client panels where clients and employees can offer praise and suggestions for product development and service improvement. Give them the chance to highlight your blind spots. There's no secret recipe to success. It takes hard work and a willingness to revolutionize the client experience. Work on turning the act of trading with you into a real experience. You can start by following these tips:

- Ensure that everyone across the organization knows how to focus on a specific person and how to be fully present while providing a service. Define how you want your clients to experience the act of trading with you, and make sure that everyone knows how to live up to that standard.
- Give all employees mental coaching to ensure adaptability. Put together an action plan for everyone in the company so that everyone becomes curious and interested in the process of developing as people and as an organization.

- Make it attractive and easy for the client to recommend your organization to other people in their network. Deliver a complete experience that they'll go home and write about on their Facebook profiles.
- Verbalize what the client should expect when they interact with your company, and make sure to hire people who excel when it comes to experiences, events, people, relationships, chemistry, and interest.
- Abolish the old division and traditional client categories. Big clients aren't necessarily the best ones. If you're going to divide clients into different categories, try something like a) loyal clients, b) established clients who show no signs of loyalty yet, and c) new clients.
- Set up a mystery service shopping experience. Pretend to be a mystery shopper within your own organization. Mystery service shopping will help you get a feel for your own abilities to be competent and service-minded all at the same time.

The organization should always keep in mind that the things their clients say and think about products, management, partners, and reputation are true. After all, the customer is always right - even in 2030.

Trend #10: Female Power
The data is clear: the clients of tomorrow are increasingly women, or those who identify as women, bringing fresh expectations to the marketplace. These clients are confident, highly informed, and demand honesty, transparency, and accountability. Organizations that recognize and adapt to this shift in demographics will be better positioned to thrive.

Consider Las Vegas as a prime example. The focus has gradually moved from gambling to entertainment and experiential offerings, reflecting broader consumer preferences. This isn't coincidental. Women and men often approach purchases differently; research shows that women tend to be experienced shoppers who value engagement and a fulfilling experience when choosing products or services.

As more women rise to leadership positions, their influence on consumer trends will continue to grow. According to a Boston Consulting Group study of 20,000 participants, women currently make over 70% of household purchasing decisions - a figure expected to rise in the coming years. Interestingly, many women report feeling underserved in several product categories, highlighting a significant opportunity for businesses to innovate and respond.

Considering this, organizations - many of which are still male-led - may benefit from deepening their understanding of their female clientele.

Here are several strategic steps to future-proof your approach:

- **Develop a Nuanced Client Insight.** Understand what drives your clients to purchase or disengage. Invest in technology, research, and product development to stay aligned with your clients' evolving needs and attitudes. Go beyond the sale; consider the deeper purpose behind each product or service you offer.

- **Foster Open Dialogue with Your Clients.** Dedicate time and resources to listening directly to your clients. Identify their core needs, rather than assuming you know them. Transparency and responsiveness to feedback can greatly enhance customer loyalty.
- **Build a Diverse Team that Reflects Your Clientele.** Hire individuals who mirror your client base as well as those who bring different perspectives. Diversity fuels innovation, but managing it effectively is essential. Organizations that succeed in aligning with diverse client needs are often rewarded with stronger growth.
- **Stay in Sync with Your Client Base.** Successful businesses anticipate shifts in their market. Cultivating a dynamic understanding of your clients allows your organization to stay relevant, adapting offerings as needs change.

As the influence of female clients continues to rise, businesses that respond thoughtfully and authentically will be well-equipped to meet the demands of the future marketplace.

Be Authentically Ambitious

Don't stop at a high rate of satisfaction. Be more ambitious. Satisfied clients aren't necessarily an indicator of overall satisfaction. Have a look at client loyalty and ambassador efforts (i.e. to know how many people your clients are recommending to your organization). All clients want to be part of something that's earned their custom. It's okay to be imperfect, so long as you're authentic and love your clients.

The focus isn't simply on optimizing internal processes; it's about building a seamless experience that makes people want to engage with your brand. Shift your investments towards your employees - empower them to become true ambassadors of your brand. This begins with reimagining customer-facing roles in sales, service, call centers, and support lines, which are often poorly compensated and undervalued. Educate, compensate, and inspire the people interacting with clients daily, transforming these touchpoints into opportunities for connection and loyalty.

Revitalize your sales approach by making client satisfaction everyone's responsibility, across every department and level. Basics like delivery guarantees and quality assurance are no longer differentiators; they're merely your ticket to entry. The organizations that thrive will be those that make the customer experience their collective purpose, aligning every policy, process, and interaction around client benefit.

Every policy you implement should be explainable with, "The advantage for the client is that...." Make it easy for clients to work with you and even easier for them to recommend you. Hire people with strong interpersonal skills and give them the freedom to create lasting, meaningful connections with clients. Your website, online store, and overall customer journey should be designed for simplicity - from first contact to potential closure. Eliminate unnecessary hurdles and excessive contracts; forget about trying to "own" a client. Instead, aim to earn them through trust and value.

Build Lasting Relationships
Treat critical clients like VIPs. Address their concerns quickly, personally, and effectively. Each year, companies lose millions due to a lack of strategy for managing dissatisfied clients. These critiques can be transformed into valuable insights and growth opportunities for your organization. Educate every team member to foster a mindset that embraces challenges, signaling to clients that they're in capable hands and that your team truly wants to help.

Consider moving beyond the term "client" to words like "member" or "partner," underscoring the idea that your relationship is collaborative. Equip your employees to communicate effectively with clients in all settings - whether in person, by phone, or online. Develop strategies for handling difficult interactions that can turn even the most critical situations into opportunities for loyalty and trust-building. Encourage employees to share experiences, good and bad, fostering a culture of continuous learning.

Build a Strong Network and Stay Relevant
Your market position depends on a strong, well-maintained network - one that takes time and intention to build. Sales and marketing have evolved tremendously over the years; survival now depends on spotting emerging trends and strategically expanding your network to drive sales.

Do You Have Ideas to Share?
If you have insights, suggestions, or ideas that deserve exploration, feel free to send them my way at sg@soulaima.dk.

I'll do my best to incorporate them into the next edition of this book.

Enjoy the journey of making your brand one that clients are not only loyal to but excited to champion.

www.ingramcontent.com/pod-product-compliance
Lightning Source LLC
Chambersburg PA
CBHW071034240526
45469CB00006BD/2210